From
SUGAR BEETS
TO
SHANGHAI

HOW AN IDAHO FARM BOY BUILT
AN INTERNATIONAL BUSINESS

GLADE POULSEN

From Sugar Beets to Shanghai
How an Idaho Farm Boy Build a Global Business
Glade Poulsen

All rights reserved. This book contains material protected under International and Federal Copyright Laws and Treaties. Any unauthorized reprint or use of this material is prohibited. No part of this book may be reproduced or transmitted in any form or by any means, electronic or mechanical, including photocopying, recording, or by any information storage and retrieval system without express written permission from the author.

© 2018 Glade Poulsen

ISBN: 9781796989212

Editor: Art Fogartie
Cover and Interior: Lisa Thomson

DEDICATION

This book is dedicated to my family.

Starting with my great-grandfather, you have braved the unknown, endured hardships, battled failure, refused to quit, pressed on in the face of abandonment, and forged towards the hope of a better tomorrow. Great-grandparents, parents, children, and grandchildren, I cherish, love, and admire you all.

This book does not happen without you. And, without you, nothing really matters.

Cindy, my rock and my heart, you see more in me than anyone else—more than I can even imagine. You know my blind spots and my shortcomings. You love me when I fail and pull me to shore when I flounder. Your grace sustains me. Your love inspires me.

CONTENTS

Chapter

1. Life on the Farm 1
2. The Closest I'll Ever Get to the Super Bowl 9
3. Danish Anyone? 17
4. Getting Started 23
5. Rise and Fall 29
6. A New Start 35
7. Arizona Dawn 39
8. The Elevator Goes Both Ways 43
9. Introduction to MLM 51
10. The Worst Financial Mistake of My Life 55
11. Hope Rises in the East 59
12. Things Are Looking Up 67
13. The Darkness 71
14. The Bottom of the Pit 77
15. Clawing Back Up 83
16. The Merger 87
17. Cruisin' Along 97
18. Tumbling Down 101

19	A Decade Lost	103
20	Half-full or Half-empty?	109
21	No Such Word	111
Epilogue		119
Acknowledgements		121

FOREWORD

I did not want to tell this story, even though a great many have asked.

I am a backrow guy—the fellow who occupies the seat farthest from the front while others command the stage. The more limelight they get, the better I like it.

I prefer to be discreet about my life—and quiet about whatever I may have been able to accomplish.

But, as I said, a lot of people asked.

This is a story of pursuit—my pursuit of a dream. In *Think and Grow Rich*, Napoleon Hill comments: "Whatever the mind can conceive, and believe, it will achieve."

I'm not quite to the goal yet—my final chapters have yet to be written. But, I'd like to share as much of my journey as I can—as much as you'd care to read.

I hope this small volume will inspire you—at least with the thought, "Well, if Glade can do it, why not me?" I do not want you to be content to have a dream; I want you to live the dream.

There are no shortcuts. If you reach your dream without obstacles, then your aspiration was not lofty enough—you sold yourself short. The things that come to us easily—without cost—seldom mean as much as the ones for which we have to struggle.

Challenges make us grow.

If that sounds trite, so be it. Your character—your true self—finds development and definition in the hours of your life when despair and defeat seem not only close, but also inevitable. The first bench-press is easy. The first set of presses may not be much more difficult. But, when (metaphorically or in reality) your muscles scream and your pulse throbs…when the sinews in your arms spasm and your eyelids twitch as you feel the bar slipping in your perspiration-slicked, sore hands… when the weights seem to resist and Gravity reaches out a leaden Hand to pull the burden back towards your heaving chest…that is when you find out if you have what Tom Wolfe called "The Right Stuff"—what Charles Portis labeled "True Grit"—what the Cowardly Lion wanted: "Courage"—what the ancients described as "gravitas."

We all have challenges. And we all occasionally lose either confidence or hope. But, we also always have a choice…up or down…left or right…forward or retreat…and, ultimately, push on or quit.

When you finish this book, I hope your determination will be, "Whatever comes—I will never give up on my dream."

– Glade Poulsen

CHAPTER 1
LIFE ON THE FARM

"Daddy are we poor?"

I vividly remember my sister's constant question.

And I vividly remember my father's consistent reply, "No, baby, we're not poor. We just don't have any money."

Farming is hard.

Family farming is harder.

Family farming in southern Idaho borders on the brutal.

Eighty acres—3,484,800 square feet. Sounds like the Ponderosa, doesn't it? In reality, it was a small spread and Dad had to work a second job just to pay the bills and put food in everyone's mouth.

There were eight of us children—and we all had responsibilities. As we grew older, the tasks got harder and proved more critical to the success of the operation. It wasn't always fun. I'm not going to blow smoke and say we all "whistled while we worked," We were kids—we would rather have been doing something else—probably *anything* else. But, now, every one of us looks back on our younger days with pride and the understanding that we learned the value of hard work.

I learned something else. I learned the difference between work that can be fun and work that makes me want to stand in front of an International Harvester. Truth is, when it is productive and fulfilling, it ceases to be work—it becomes fun.

Because of my younger days, I now know that when I am engaged in something that is boring and unchallenging (even if it may be profitable), it is time to move on to something else.

Sugar beets go in the ground before April 6. Idaho weather is "interesting" to say the least. But in most cases, there were a few good weeks in the early spring when we could prepare the soil, fertilize it until it's just so, and plant. The beets went down in rows—precise lines dug in the earth—which looked like they'd been laid out by a mathematician.

Once we "got the plants in," it snowed—if we were lucky. That last coat of powder replenished the water content in the soil (we had to have relatively dry conditions for optimum planting). With the proper moisture content, new seedlings did not have to struggle quite so mightily to break through the Earth's outer crust in their search for light and heat.

If we got rain instead of snow, the ground got a little like a graham cracker you left in your lunch box too long—brown, dry, and hard. When the rains came, we had to take a culti-mulcher and break up the soil to help the seedlings in their journey. The work was delicate—too fast or too much "umph" could root up the seedlings. You can't just chop away in a newly planted field like you are surrounded by gophers and you're in a contest to see how many you can behead.

You couldn't disturb the seed bed—else all was lost.

Of course, weather being fickle, sometimes it would neither rain nor snow, and the ground threatened to turn into pottery. We had to roll out the sprinkler line and water everything. You can't flood the plants—you can't cheat the plants of water. It takes thought…concentration… and practice.

Farming taught me about work—and about unpredictability. Things will always go according to plan—except when they don't. So, along with all the other lessons, I learned a lot about flexibility. There are a lot of variables in farming—you never know what's going to happen.

There are a lot more variables in life. Only Hollywood can script life—the stuff you and I experience comes at us in wild, varied, different, tangential, and, sometimes, inconceivable patterns.

The weather goes wrong, the planting is screwed up. The planting goes right, something happens at the time of the harvest. You have the biggest and best harvest of all times, circumstances completely beyond anything you can ever control cause the market to go into the tank and you are left with a fabulous crop of sugar beets *that no one wants to buy*.

Life leads us on a serpentine path. Sometimes you screw up and everything miraculously works in your favor. Sometimes, you do everything right, and at the precise moment when you should be on top of the world, you experience a crash and burn that makes the Hindenburg disaster look like a marshmallow roast.

What the farm and my father taught me was to get up and face adversity. Moping and self-pity serve no purpose. How we face adversity—what we do in the face of difficulty—separates successful people from the unsuccessful. I heard Dad's favorite saying all the time after a disastrous hail storm or a sea of red ink in the book: "There's always next year."

I lived in Arizona for twenty-five years and I visited the Grand Canyon whenever I could. That marvelous scar in the Earth came from eons of wind, storm, flood, and scorching heat. Nature's abuse carved the magnificence people from all over the world still come to see.

We will probably never exhibit such astounding beauty, but you and I absolutely will bear the mark of every storm we endure, every blow we absorb, every failure we endure, every knee we skin to the bone, and every tear we shed.

Lesson One: the greatest thing you can ever own is—*experience*.

Experiences and trials mold us—shaping us into beautifully unique characters. If everything comes easily to you, you may never completely appreciate your gifts. Ownership rises from struggle. No one likes difficulty—in fact, it stinks. But the confidence that bursts into bloom following the heavy seas of a torturous experience glazes your life with a strong and resistant sheen of character.

Dad never pushed us or tried to instill a desire in me. If I saw a bigger tractor, I wanted to learn to drive it. One year, I insisted on planting the sugar beets—driving the tractor that pulled the planter through the furrows into which the seeds fell. I am now convinced Dad knew the outcome before the key turned on the ignition for the first time but telling me I couldn't do something was not his way—ever.

He was next to me, watching, ensuring I hadn't bitten off too big a bite.

We had a neighbor whose farm should have graced the cover and pages of every agricultural magazine in the country. Pristine rows seemingly laid out by some divine geometry wizard. Today, laser-guided tractors move in sweet precision like they are on rails. Back then, it was hard work and experience-driven talent.

The year I ran the tractor, a machine held together with bailing wire, spit, bubble gum and anything else gooey we could find, I did my absolute best.

The front wheels wobbled—made steering a little inexact. Even the most experienced planter would have struggled mightily given the dilapidated condition of the machine. I did my best. And when I finished, the rows upon which I gazed with such pride looked…like a sidewinder snake had carved the furrows with his wiggling backside.

The neighbor stopped by to speak to Dad. He leaned out of the window of his new Ford pickup, chin resting on his folded arms, his sunglasses raised a little to allow a better view of my maiden planting endeavor. Dad sat on the tailgate of his old GMC, his arm resting on a seed sack.

The neighbor said, "Rex, you gonna dig those back up and replant tomorrow?"

Dad studied the situation, giving thought, no doubt, to the intricacies of maintaining such squiggles and zigzags. Surely his trained eye saw every problem the "unique" layout would present for irrigation and air flow—the issues that would arise during harvest as pickers tried to navigate rows that seemed to run in all four compass directions at once.

Dad looked, stood, hitched his pants, and said, "Sam, I'm not raising sugar beets. I'm raising a boy."

My second lesson: Skill comes from doing.

Haven't mention Mother much. She died from breast cancer one week short of my seventh birthday. I don't have a lot of memories. Everyone tells me she was a wonderful person, an individual full of love and compassion—someone who put others before herself. Since I believe in the Hereafter, I have great confidence of reuniting with her someday.

The diagnosis came two years earlier, but even after the surgeon's blade took both her breasts, the Man with the Sickle continued to stalk her. Medicine has made great strides in the treatment of this dread disease, but we have a long way to go before we find a cure for this plague that attacks one in every eight women. I still feel her influence as if she is standing on the other side of a waspish vail, whispering to me, guiding me, encouraging me in every good thing I do.

After the mastectomy, the insurance cancelled my parents' coverage, so they went without insurance until the end. After surgery, Mom underwent chemotherapy with the understanding that the disease might rear its ugly head again in two years.

Twenty-four months later, as if on some sort of malevolent timer, the disease reappeared. Without any insurance, Mom didn't last long.

What little treatment she got was devastatingly expensive. Dad remortgaged the farm. Neither of my parents ever said a word about the situation. Mom would not let us see her lying down. Dad never talked about the crushing financial burden under which he staggered. He did not express any animosity towards the insurance company.

He just faced each day of challenge and worked through it as best he could. My uncle came up with a scheme to help us. He was entrepreneurial, so Dad leveraged himself a little more (most farmers live on the edge anyway), bought a bunch of younger cattle, heifers that would become milk cows after they calved. We grew alfalfa to feed the cattle as they grew into maturity—approaching the time for breeding.

We didn't sell any crops; we kept them to fatten the cows. Heifer prices had been remarkably stable, and my uncle had done quite well for a while. We all pitched in—we fed those cows all the time…in the scorching heat and in the bone-chattering cold. No matter how we felt, what we planned, what we wanted to do—we fed those cows twice a day—365 days a year.

The plan was great.

The plan should have worked.

The plan didn't.

Just as we were preparing to take the cattle to market, the price bottomed out. We sold the cows, but we couldn't cover the note.

Dad never complained.

And he never quit. "There's always next year."

Dad had another saying. "No such word as can't, son." If he said it to me once, he said it 10,000 times. Babies don't learn to walk if they stay on their backsides the first time they wobble out of balance. Baseball players never learn to hit if they walk off the field the first time they miss a pitch.

While some people might suggest that farmers never learn, period, I'm here to tell you that the people who wrestle our food from the Earth are the toughest, most stubborn, hardest working, most optimistic, "can do" people God ever put on the planet.

And I am proud I learned at the feet of one of the best.

CHAPTER 2
THE CLOSEST I'LL EVER GET TO THE SUPER BOWL

Doug Bingham and Blaine Atkinson. Not exactly Lawrence Taylor and John Riggins, but they stood at the focal point of the biggest event of my football life.

I was the youngest of eight. Mom died when I was six, so we all grew up faster than we would have preferred. We divided the cooking, cleaning, housework, and whatever love and tenderness were required. I was the punching bag and the "go-fer." "Glade go fer this…go fer that." If I didn't, there was the punching bag business again.

To survive, I became competitive, so when the time arrived, I was ready, willing, and eager for sports. Dad was working his behind off, so I learned my sports from my older brothers and my sports philosophy from the ABC Network's *Wide World of Sports*. I listened every week as Jim McKay touted, "The thrill of victory," and I watched in recurring horror as Vinko Bogataj from Slovenia crashed at the bottom of his ski jump attempt to be described, once again, as "The agony of defeat."

All of my brothers were very good athletes. We always were very involved with each season and each sport at our small high school. For more than 20 years, Dad came to every home game and a lot of the ones out of town. Sometimes, the drive was 2-3 hours. He was supportive and each of us has commented across the years about how much his quiet attendance meant to us.

He never said much. But, he was there—much more important.

By the time I was a junior, we did not have a lot of experience—or talent. The year before, we competed on the JV level. We were a Class III school. We had a newly-minted coach. He might have been out of college for 18 minutes. "Miserable" does not accurately describe our ineptitude. We lost the first game 54-0. I don't remember the score of any of the other games my junior year, but I remember the results.

We were perfect…0 and 12.

The next year, those of us who'd gotten our faces stomped every Friday night as juniors at least had some experience. And, not surprisingly, we had a new coach—a young man who'd been a great athlete at Utah State University.

We wondered how we got him. In truth, it was probably the only job available, but he never acted that way. He worked us like we were Lombardi's Packers, or Stram's Chiefs, or the Bear's Crimson Tide. He worked on instilling confidence in us.

His attention to detail was marvelous to behold. No matter was too small or too insignificant, from ensuring the coolers were full before the game to making sure every player had a back-up pair of shoe strings.

We started winning—we started beating bigger schools. We ended up playing in the regional conference championship game. There was no state championship at the time.

The game was in the Mini-Dome, at the time the only domed stadium on any western college campus. This was big time. We wore basketball shoes instead of cleats…we stared at the enormous scoreboard and flinched whenever someone spoke over the mountainous sound system.

It was as close as any of us would ever get to the Super Bowl. We were the West Side Pirates…and we were down three points with 37 seconds left—the other team had the ball. The season was over—a good one—but not the ending we'd wanted.

Our defense held—4th down. I knew I would drop back to return the punt. In the huddle, Doug Bingham, a wiry kid who played middle linebacker was acting like he was having a stroke. His eyes were dilated. He was panting. His jaw was clenched, and he kept pounding his hand into his fist.

I dropped back, ready to look for my lane—determined to take the ball the distance. My view of what happened was perfect. Doug timed the snap perfectly. He was a fraction of a second off the ball before anyone else moved. He broke through the line without any resistance, flung himself into the air, blocked the punt, and recovered the ball on the 21-yard line.

Pandemonium.

Coach called time. We were ready for our best play—power sweep left—Tim Sant, our fabulous halfback would take it to the house.

"I, right—32 hitch—halfback fake—halfback pass."

Blaine Atkinson, a wall of a human being, had blocked for Tim all season. I think Blaine might have touched the ball during a game once—by accident. Now, he was the focal point of the most important play we would run all year.

No one spoke. No one objected. "Ready—break." We clapped and trotted out to the field. We knew the play—we'd run it every day in practice. We'd never even thought about it during a game.

The QB took the snap and pitched it to Tim who scooted left with the ball tucked under his arm. He looked for all the world like a kid intent on running the ball into the end zone 63 feet away. Suddenly, Tim pulled to a stop, stood erect, and tossed a wobbly spiral into the left corner of the end zone where Blaine Atkinson stood—absolutely alone.

He caught the only touchdown pass of his career.

Come to think of it, the punt was the only one Doug Bingham ever blocked in his life.

But, those guys were part of a team—a unit—a corps whose members were more dedicated to the success of the unit than they were to the opportunity for individual accolades. The most surprising part of the story for me is not that the unknown players came through, but that the guys who, by all rights, should have been the stars, never did anything other than congratulate the hell out of their "one hit wonder" teammates.

Our school was too small to field a baseball team so, after basketball season, we had track. I ran on the mile relay team—four guys, one lap each, flat out. When you neared the end of your loop, you passed a baton to the next guy who took off like his pants were on fire. The second fastest guy ran lead-off…and the "streak" handled the anchor (last) position. Makes sense…get out to a lead…hand it over to two guys who could hold their own…and let the last guy either blow the field away or come from behind for a glorious victory.

At least, that's the theory.

Mac ran first. With a loping stride and long, prematurely thinning hair that bounced as he ran, Mac almost always had us in first or second position by the first baton exchange. Races live and die in the passing zone. The exchange has to be clean and within the boundaries; otherwise, your squad can be disqualified or lose precious time.

We practiced the exchange every day until I think we could have done it blindfolded.

We knew the run-in distance and the time it took each one of us to get there, "Go," and the next man would sprint towards the first marker. "Reach"—the shout from the racer telling the next man to extend his arm back in preparation to feel the 50-gram, 28-centimeter baton.

When done correctly, it is a thing of beauty.

When you screw it up, you feel like you are standing in the middle of the track—naked.

We qualified for the State Track Meet at Boise State University—we were the only part of our school's team to make it. We'd never been to the state capital before. For a bunch of farm boys, the place looked enormous.

The meet started in the morning, but our event was not until early afternoon. The closer we got to "show time," the queasier we all got. We huddled on the infield grass with our arms on each other's shoulders.

"We're lucky to be here."

"Not everybody gets this chance."

"Let's do the best we can."

"Leave it all on the track—we've only got this one race."

In a made-for-tv, afternoon movie, we would have stormed up from last place and won the race in a photo finish. That didn't happen. But, we did run our very best. Two of us ran so hard that we puked in the bushes when we were finished.

We did not win—we finished fifth. I'm sorry—*we finished FIFTH!* No, we didn't place. We didn't go home with medals or ribbons or trophies, but we held our heads high. We were the fifth best mile relay team in the Great State of Idaho.

To this day, we are all proud of the heart and determination we exhibited.

It's not always about being first. It is always about doing everything you can to excel. When you bust your butt—when you do everything you can after preparing as diligently as you can—then whatever happens is a tribute to your effort.

Get Up and Win the Race

Whenever I start to hang my head in front of failure's face, my downward fall is broken by the memory of a race.

A children's race, young boys, young men; how I remember well, excitement sure, but also fear, it wasn't hard to tell.

They all lined up so full of hope, each thought to win that race or tie for first, or if not that, at least take second place.

Their parents watched from off the side, each cheering for their son, and each boy hoped to show his folks that he would be the one.

The whistle blew and off they flew, like chariots of fire, to win, to be the hero there, was each young boy's desire.

One boy in particular, whose dad was in the crowd, was running in the lead and thought "My dad will be so proud."

But as he speeded down the field and crossed a shallow dip, the little boy who thought he'd win, lost his step and slipped.

Trying hard to catch himself, his arms flew everyplace, and midst the laughter of the crowd he fell flat on his face.

As he fell, his hope fell too; he couldn't win it now.

Humiliated, he just wished to disappear somehow.

But as he fell his dad stood up and showed his anxious face, which to the boy so clearly said, "Get up and win that race!"

He quickly rose, no damage done, behind a bit that's all, and ran with all his mind and might to make up for his fall.

So anxious to restore himself, to catch up and to win, his mind went faster than his legs. He slipped and fell again.

He wished that he had quit before with only one disgrace.
"I'm hopeless as a runner now, I shouldn't try to race."

But through the laughing crowd he searched and found his
father's face with a steady look that said again, "Get up and
win that race!"
So, he jumped up to try again, ten yards behind the last.
"If I'm to gain those yards," he thought, "I've got to run real fast!"

Exceeding everything he had, he regained eight, then ten...
but trying hard to catch the lead, he slipped and fell again.
Defeat! He lay there silently. A tear dropped from his eye.
"There's no sense running anymore! Three strikes I'm out!
Why try?

I've lost, so what's the use?" he thought. "I'll live with my disgrace."
But then he thought about his dad, who soon he'd have to face.
"Get up," an echo sounded low, "you haven't lost at all, for all
you have to do to win is rise each time you fall.
"Get up!" the echo urged him on, "Get up and take your place!
"You were not meant for failure here! Get up and win that race!"

So, up he rose to run once more, refusing to forfeit, and he
resolved that win or lose, at least he wouldn't quit.
So far behind the others now, the most he'd ever been, still he
gave it all he had and ran like he could win.
Three times he'd fallen stumbling, three times he rose again.
Too far behind to hope to win, he still ran to the end.

They cheered another boy who crossed the line and won first
place, head high and proud and happy—no falling, no disgrace.
But, when the fallen youngster crossed the line, in last place,
the crowd gave him a greater cheer for finishing the race.
And even though he came in last with head bowed low,

unproud, you would have thought he'd won the race, to listen to the crowd.
And to his dad he sadly said, "I didn't do so well."

"To me, you won," his father said. "You rose each time you fell."
And now when things seem dark and bleak and difficult to face, the memory of that little boy helps me in my own race.
For all of life is like that race, with ups and downs and all.
And all you have to do to win is rise each time you fall.
And when depression and despair shout loudly in my face, another voice within me says, "Get up and win that race!"

~ Attributed to Dr. D.H. "Dee" Groberg

CHAPTER 3
DANISH ANYONE?

In the Church of Jesus Christ of Latter-Day Saints young men (age nineteen) and women (age twenty) who express a willingness to serve the Church, submit paperwork stating they will go anywhere in the world on a two-year mission.

My family hails from Denmark. At a young age, my grandmother joined the Church and left Denmark. Her father never saw nor talked to her again.

Still, she loved her native land and dreamed that one of her sons or grandsons would visit Denmark as a missionary. My grandmother died three months before I turned 19. I don't know why, but something told me I would be serving among the Danes.

"Keep your emotions in check," Dad said. "You don't want to be too disappointed if you end up someplace less exotic—like Montana,"

"But," I told him with arrogance, "I don't even have to open the letter. I know I'm going there."

The postman knew what was in the envelope, so he honked the horn when he pulled in front of the house. We'd probably only asked him *every day* if there was a letter from the Church.

"No need for me to look," I said. "I know I'm going to Denmark."

I handed the letter to Dad and said, "Open it." I watched his eyes move back and forth—and the smile beginning at the ends of his mouth. Then, he said, "Darn, kid."

He handed the letter to my stepmother. She read the note aloud, "You have been called to serve your mission in Copenhagen, Denmark."

I reported to the Language Training Center in Rexburg, Idaho where I took a two-month crash course in Danish. When the plane's wheels folded into the fuselage on the way over, I thought I was pretty fluent, a determination I held right up until the time we de-planed and I heard the people in the Kastrup Airport.

I was sure the pilot had missed the target by several thousand miles. These people could not possibly be speaking Danish—I did not understand a word!

Some other missionaries met me and showed me around the city. They wanted to keep me awake until my body clock adjusted. The next morning, they put me on a train for an eight-hour journey to the southern-most part of Jutland, right next to the German border. I had never felt more lost and alone. What had I done?

Until now, the biggest adventure of my life had been to Boise. Now I was half a world away and pledged to stay here with these people (who *obviously* do not speak Danish) for two long years.

The experience was marvelous. Like most new things, the first few months were thrilling. After the "new car smell" wore off, the assignment was tough—and sometimes tedious. We walked all day, knocked on doors, and asked people if they were interested in hearing about our Church.

Most of the time, with very rare exceptions, the people declined. People laughed and pointed at us as we pedaled our bikes through town. (Little did I know what kind of preparation I was getting for entry into the multi-level marketing world of my later life.)

When someone finally consented to let us in, it was exhilarating. Speaking to people, heart-to-heart, in another language was a great experience.

Still, constant rejection wears on you. I talked to myself—a lot. *What was I thinking?*

If I had thought I would make it, I would have swum home.

Being away from everything and everyone was hard. A lot of the guys I knew were back in college with girlfriends…and fun…and football games…and, did I mention, girlfriends. I was wearing a white shirt and a black tie, poor, struggling to converse in a foreign language, and facing ridicule. And I *volunteered* for this!

Nonetheless, after about eight months, I lost myself in the work. I forgot about myself and devoted my time to serving others. All of a sudden, it was nearly time to leave. I could express myself fluently in the native tongue, I had met relatives and walked the same streets that my grandmother had trod as a girl.

She was a talented pianist and organist. From a very young age, she played in the stunning Lutheran cathedrals in Copenhagen. She was accepted at the Julliard School of Music in the U.K.

That's why her father disowned her—she threw away a future in music—her great gift—for some "weird, new, American church."

My faith grew, and my self-assuredness exploded. I knew I was doing the right thing for me and for others. I believed in what I was doing.

When you lose yourself in the service of others, when you concentrate on the things outside of yourself, love for life and work grows.

After twenty-four months, I had mixed feelings. Part of me wanted to stay. I didn't have a career in the States—I didn't have a fiancée—I knew I always had a place with my folks, but I did not have my own home. For two years, I had not been required to make a single decision—now I would be responsible for everything.

Looking back, as I still do often, I am so grateful for that experience. I learned fundamentals for success that I continue to employ—

endurance, service, discipline, faith, deep-seated belief in a project, tolerance, salesmanship, communication/listening skills, empathy, structure, personal growth, personal study, understanding and more.

Not everyone can or should go on a religious mission. But, I am convinced those two years away from everything I previously knew helped set me on a course to success and I would encourage every young person to replicate my youthful journey in some way.

***

My mission opportunity turned me onto a whole new concept of personal growth and development—I don't even think it was a category anyone ever considered in 1973.

I'd never been out of Idaho. Now, at nineteen, I was with 150 missionaries. Some were my contemporaries. Some were "old men" at twenty-five. Most of them were from America, but there were a few from Denmark, Finland and Germany.

We were nothing if not eager. We all wanted to serve, to learn and to succeed. I didn't know any better, so I was brimming with the confidence (arrogance?) of youth. I wasn't afraid of competition. One of my brothers had been to Norway on his mission. If he could conquer Scandinavia, I knew I could.

We served the entire country. There was a Mission President who chose his assistants to be his "right hand men." The mission was divided into three geographic zones—two leaders per zone—each zone broken into four to five districts. The Assistants worked directly with the President, then passed instruction and direction to the Zone Leaders who "moved the water downstream" to the District Leaders.

One of the Assistants had been in Denmark exactly one year longer than I had. He was sharp, articulate and walked faster than any human being I had ever met. Bob Whitman was one talented guy.

He had charisma out the ying-yang, could recite reams of poetry, knew the Scriptures like the back of his hand, spoke fluent Danish and had a gift for communication. He'd suspended his college football career to go on his mission.

He impressed me—I wanted to be like him. I didn't play football anymore, but I longed for his knowledge and "smooth." At a conference, I approached him.

"How do you do it?" I asked.

After he figured out what I was talking about, he said, "You have to be willing to sacrifice."

"Sacrifice what?"

"Time. I get up a half hour earlier than everyone else. I spend the time learning something new."

Farm boys don't have any trouble with early rising and I told him so.

"Cool," he said. "Visualize yourself as confident—not cocky or arrogant—but confident. Believe in yourself."

Check.

"Read good material every day. Memorize the information. I use 3x5 cards—I put them in a recipe box and review them constantly—fifteen minutes a day, three times a day."

"The Box" became my first tool for personal growth and development. I started using it the very next day—and kept it up for the balance of my mission. I memorized an entire scripture guide book, Danish vocabulary, poetry and I could give our presentations to prospective members word for word without notes.

Later in my mission, when I was a District, then Zone, Leader, I taught others how to utilize the box. Our Zone became notorious for the boxes in our zones. Whenever there was a zone competition, we kicked butt. I have used the box my entire business life. It is an incredible tool for learning.

When I needed to pass the real estate test in Arizona, I used the box. Forty years later, the box got me through the contractors' exam in both Idaho and Utah.

I also met the late Grant Ipsen. He was the President. Pres. Ipsen was a young, energetic master salesperson with MONY (Mutual of New York Insurance Company). Being from a small town near Preston, Idaho, famous from the movie *Napoleon Dynamite* (and yes, I knew practically every house and all the stores in the film) I was a real rube in Copenhagen. Pornographic pictures and sex shops abounded: lewd newspapers, magazines, books and tabloids hit me at every turn. I had never seen anything like it and it bothered me because I was trying to focus on religious matters.

I asked Grant how to control my mind. He laughed and recited an old Danish proverb. Translated to English, it goes something like this:

> *You cannot prevent a raven from flying over your chimney, but you can prevent the raven from building a nest there.*

We will encounter negative thoughts, criticism, doubts, fears and insecurities, but we can determine whether they will control our minds.

"Whenever you have a negative or inappropriate thought," he said, "Think about something else. Whistle a tune, recite a poem, sing a song—just get your mind going in a different direction."

I learned to move my mind in positive directions. Later, when I lost my way, I had to relearn the lessons from my mission.

But, at least I had something from my past to use in my self-rescue.

CHAPTER 4
GETTING STARTED

Three months out of college, the ink still a little wet on the diploma, I got married to Laura. We were young, innocent, and probably figured since we were from the same county, liked each other's families and knew a lot of the same people, the marriage thing was a good idea.

I was always told to choose a career that would be fun. Sounded reasonable. I enjoyed athletics in school, and understood the philosophies of football, basketball and track. I decided to be a coach. I applied everywhere I could find—I was going to be the next Bear Bryant or John Wooden.

Not exactly.

The best offer I received was a job handing out towels at the Recreation Center for $3.50 an hour. Seriously—you should have seen the ones I rejected. *This is what I get for a bachelor's degree?*

Back up a minute…

The previous summer, I had completed an internship—40 hours a week for eight weeks, for credits towards graduating. No pay—only credit towards graduation. In the evenings, I umpired in the city softball league for $5.00 per game. I also worked weekends in the produce section of a local grocery store.

At the end of two months, I did not have much money and I wondered how I was going to pay for my last year's tuition, housing and living expenses. I loaded my little Datsun B-210 and headed for Houston, Texas with $86 in my pocket. My sister told me I could live with her for a few weeks. My older brother, who was not much of a salesman, had just made several thousand dollars selling pots and pans. I figured, *if Rod can do it, I can make twice as much in half the time.*

I took off, not knowing if eighty-six dollars would last until I hit south Texas.

It did—barely.

In Houston, I met someone who changed my life—Stan Knickerbocker, a consummate salesman. He could sell "slither" to a snake.

He gave me ten sets of cookware and went out with me to show me how to sell them. I went door-to-door. I would walk into a title company and ask the ladies, "You in the market for some great pots and pans?"

I showed them the seven-piece set (list price $69.95). "Look at this," I said, scraping a quarter across the frying pan to show the scratch-resistant features of the T-Fal finish. Then, in a lower voice, I said, "What would you say to … $29.95 … for the whole lot?" That was my pitch. Every stinking time.

But, Stan showed me a better way. He had a different story—for every occasion.

I watched him—and I learned.

"Folks," he said, "We just closed a show at the Marriott and I have seventy sets of these pots and pans left over. It will cost me more to send them back to Pennsylvania than it is worth, so I am selling these sets at my absolute cost. I'm going store-to-store until I sell every last one of them."

He showed the brochure—rubbed the quarter—dropped the pan in someone's hand from a few inches above their hands (to make it seem heavier) and verbally created the image that these products were extra-heavy duty and extra-high quality.

Another story he liked: "I just bought my wife a brand-new Buick Electra 225 and she told me that she was not going to have her brand-new car sit out on the driveway one more night. She insists that I get rid of these last seventy sets of pot and pans, so she can park her baby in the garage. So, I'm selling these at a loss. You know—'If Mama isn't happy—no one is happy!'"

In truth, Stan had railroad cars of pots and pans delivered every month—partially because he sold so dadgum many of them.

After watching Stan for a few hours, I was on my own with a car full of pots and pans. Stan consigned ten sets to me and said I could sell them and then build up to the point where I would own my own inventory. I paid $15.00 per set to Stan. Whatever I got over and above the $15 was mine—all mine.

I started using the "Marriott pitch." My first day, I sold two sets. The next day—a grueling ten hours of rejection after rejection, I sold four. My conscience started to pinch a little—I knew I wasn't telling the truth. I didn't even know where the Marriott was.

Every time I started talking, I could feel the blinking neon sign on my forehead and hear the old song by the Castaways: *Liar, liar, pants on fire—your nose is longer than a telephone wire.*

I finally decided to take a radical step—I would tell the truth.

I changed my sales pitch and told the people I was a college student from Idaho here for the balance of the summer. I needed to make money for school by selling these great pots and pans. "These list for $69.95, but I bought them for a substantially discounted rate. I will sell them to you, for my sister has a set and uses them every day. She really likes them." (She did, and it was the truth.)

I did the demonstration with the quarter and handed the pan to them, so they could test the weight. Even when I handed it over gently, they commented on how heavy it felt.

I closed with, "They come in almond, avocado green, and chocolate, which one would you like?"

The first day of the new-improved-honest Glade, I sold *every single set in my car—ten!* By 2:00 PM, I had made $125. In three weeks, I made over $3,000 and had enough money to pay for my last two quarters of college.

What a lesson! *The truth is good enough!* Too often, sales managers and trainers teach trickery and gimmicks—whatever it takes to get the sale. I promise, the truth is always the best way.

MLM has a great business model—one in which I believe. It is not a get rich quick scheme, but it has created a lot of millionaires.

Is it easy? Absolutely not, but it is worth it. Our model puts fantastic products in consumers' hands in a fast and efficient way. Why do we have to make up stories—or embellish our incomes? We don't.

The truth is good enough.

Don't tell people you are making more money than you are. Don't tell people you are bigger than you are. In the beginning, I used my mentor's proof of income to show what was possible and that I had faith and confidence in the system. Then, I showed my own earnings to demonstrate the truth and reality of my situation—I knew I could replicate the success other people enjoyed—but only if I was willing to pay the price.

We shoot ourselves in the foot when we say this business is easy. It isn't. If it were easy, everyone would be doing it.

Always tell the truth.

Back to the story…

Since I was not enthused about a job as the towel guy, I fell back on my sales experience of the previous summer.

I slid the headphones back. "What?"

"Come with me," he said. "My parents want me to check out some possible cabin plans for the spot at Bear Lake."

"Nope," I said—well, I was probably a little more direct and a little less polite.

He lifted the needle off the spinning disk. "Let's go, Glade."

The "houses" were modular homes—and they were built in a large warehouse. We were talking to a guy named Dell Loy—funny how you remember pivotal people in life. Anyway, Dell Loy said things were going well.

"In fact," he said, "We're building a new factory—it'll triple production. We're going to hire a new sales guy as soon as it's up and running."

I was violating his personal bubble about a half-second later.

"Here I am," I said. "I'm your guy. I can start in two weeks."

"Experience in the home-selling business?"

"No, but I sold a bunch of pots and pans in Houston." I started talking fast. *When in doubt, dazzle 'em with BS.* "I made more money in three weeks than most people made in six months. I paid for my last year at school."

Dell Loy looked skeptical.

"Listen, man," I said, "I went on my mission to Denmark. I learned Danish. I was there two years—never had a convert. But, I never quit—never."

Dell Loy's eyebrows arched. "Doesn't sound like you were too convincing."

"Those guys are hard-core Lutherans. They thought I was an idiot. But, I stayed at it. And I will stay with this. No one out works me."

Dell Loy looked at my roommate, who nodded.

"You got a resume?" Dell Loy asked.

"Don't need one—besides, I've told you everything you need to know. Trust your gut. Tell me when to show up and I'll be there—I'll be early. If you don't like what you see in the first thirty days, I'll leave without a fuss—no hard feelings. It won't cost you a dime. I will outsell *everybody*, including you!" (And, I could tell that he was good.)

Not sure what had come over me—I was not a self-promoter. I think it was desperation—and the thought of the sights that would haunt me every day if I had to hand out towels.

Dell Loy shrugged. "Be here a week from next Monday—9:00 AM."

"I won't let you down."

I didn't.

I started with the new homes sales business and loved it. Right after we were married, I told Laura, "Someday, babe, I'm going to make $2000 a month doing this.

Graduation was in March. I started in April and took a little time off to get married and to honeymoon.

My first 1099 (eight months' work) exceeded $18,000.

The next year, I nearly tripled the figure.

CHAPTER 5
RISE AND FALL

We were shipping houses all over Idaho, Utah, Wyoming and parts of Nevada. The money was beyond my wildest expectations. I even surprised the owners of the company. They kept raising prices and I kept selling houses.

Unfortunately, I began to believe my own hype—I thought I was a great salesman. Little did I know how easy it is to make money in a growth environment. The situation multiplied and magnified my efforts Despite my ever-growing confidence, it wasn't me bringing the success, it was the Baby Boomer Factor.

I didn't know it then, but have since learned, of the impact boomers had on every market in America. They were the "watermelon passing through a garden hose." The enormous mass of humanity (one-third of the world's population was born between 1946 and 1964) made selling *anything* a relatively simple matter.

There were a lot of folks—and all of them needed…well…everything from homes and cars to hammers and water heaters. College was over, and I began selling homes. The leading edge of the Boomer Generation was turning thirty.

There were nowhere near enough houses in the United States. The building industry exploded. Home prices took the elevator to the top floor and stayed there. People everywhere—anywhere—could get whatever they asked for when they sold a home. It was the quintessential sellers' market. In a rampant growth environment, ordinary people can do extraordinary things. I didn't have to be good—all I had to do was show up!

A little diversion: Dr. Ken Dychtwald, Ph.D. has emerged as the nation's foremost visionary and original thinker regarding the lifestyle, marketing and workforce implications of the "age wave." He is a psychologist, gerontologist and author of ten books on aging-related issues. In 1986, he became the founding President and CEO of Age Wave, a firm created to guide Fortune 500 companies and government groups in product/service development for boomers and mature adults.

In recent years, he has served as a fellow of the World Economic Forum and is the recipient of the distinguished American Society on Aging Award for outstanding national leadership in the field of aging.

His strikingly accurate predictions have been featured in many prestigious publications including: *The New York Times, The Wall Street Journal, USA Today, The Financial Times, Fortune, Time, Newsweek, Business Week, Inc., U.S. News and World Report* and *Advertising Age.*

In his best-selling book, *Age Wave,* he goes into great detail of the *bulge* of people known as the Baby Boomers and their terrific impact on markets since the mid-1940s until now and what we can expect in the future. Any business-minded individual who wants to predict the future should read this book. It is fascinating, and it will impact the way you think about business and the moves you should make to ensure confidence in business trends and timing.

Having participated (twice) in the construction industry and now being engaged with Unicity, I can attest that your swimming speed depends entirely on whether you are with or against the current. When you are working in a growth environment, you are swimming downstream (faster with less effort). When you are working in a declining or stagnant environment, the opposite holds true (difficult, maximum effort with little or no progress always looking around looking for objects coming at you from upstream).

If you have ever walked on a moving sidewalk, imagine turning around and walking "into the motion." I believe you get my point.

Baby Boomer Generation

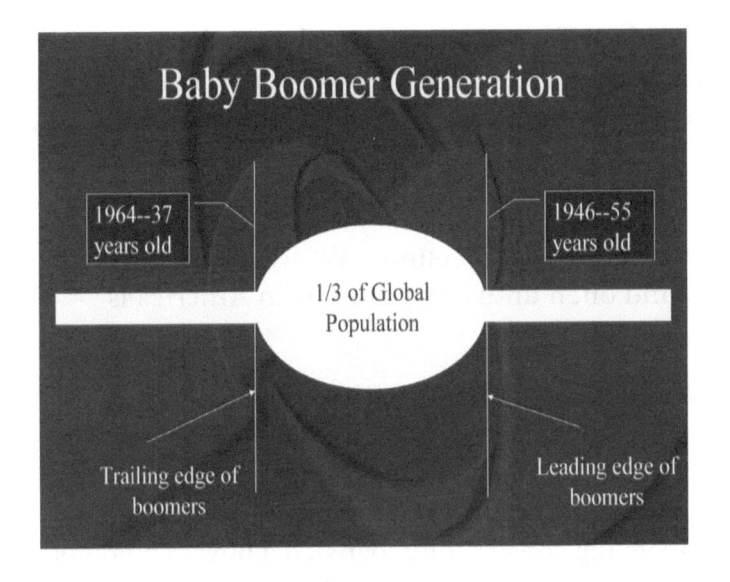

- 1964--37 years old (Trailing edge of boomers)
- 1946--55 years old (Leading edge of boomers)
- 1/3 of Global Population

I was selling homes like crazy. I could charge just about whatever I wanted because our factory could deliver! We built one home every business day. Getting a home was a snap.

A buyer would sign a contract; I would get a construction loan and order a home. I had a crew pour a foundation and wait. When the home came, there were some "tidy up" construction issues; we put in the driveways and the porches and obtained the Certificate of Occupancy. The buyers got their permanent financing, I paid off my construction loan, everyone was happy and I moved on to another sale. (Of course, I was handling multiple deals every week.) Five hundred dollars down—*five hundred*—put the construction loan contingent on the long-term financing.

Girl Scouts should have such an easy time selling cookies.

Banks loved me and buyers loved me.

I was on top of the world!

And then, disaster.

***

Everything came apart after Jimmy Carter was elected president. I'm not blaming him, but history will long remember the economic disaster of the late 70s during his four years in office.

Inflation hit the marketplace like a runaway bus. The purchasing power of the dollar shriveled. Interest rates started to rise—between 1978 and 1979, prices jumped an average of 7%! One night, Paul Volker, Chairman of the Federal Reserve, was on the television. When I heard what he said, I felt my lungs collapse.

"We are going to stop inflation in this country. We will begin raising interest rates quickly and often until every Skilsaw in America is turned off."

This farm boy from Idaho did not know squat about business, but I was getting ready to learn—the hard way. In less than six months, interest rates climbed from 7 to 17%. As rates climbed, fewer and fewer buyers could qualify for a home loan. Although I had signed contracts (and accompanying construction loans), if a buyer could not obtain permanent financing, he or she could walk away—and I was left holding the proverbial bag.

One by one, downcast buyers shuffled into the model home and canceled their contracts. When the banks inquired if I had buyers in place, I had to say "no." The minute I uttered that little syllable, the bank called the construction loan—and I had to pay.

I was over-extended. I'd bought lots and paid for foundations—homes were ready for occupants. But, there were no buyers. While I was not the only builder in trouble, I surely felt alone. Banks foreclosed on home builders right and left.

I was in the deep end of the pool trying to dog paddle with a cinder block tied to each leg.

There was more bad news—in fact, much worse.

I'd talked my oldest brother into joining me in the business. He was in there battling as hard as he could.

Despite the struggles of a great many Americans, farmers were killing it. Laura's father sold farm equipment—and I saw a chance to keep from drowning.

To my everlasting shame, I left my brother to fend for himself—which he did heroically—and started as a salesman in my father-in-law's business.

My brother has forgiven me—multiple times—but I still carry the shame.

CHAPTER 6
A NEW START

Although I developed a lot of new clients for my father-in-law, and I made very good money selling farm machinery, it just did not speak to me. It was "their" business. My wife's brother assumed control and became the third-generation owner. He was fantastic—genuine, authentic and smart. It was his calling. (Now, his son runs the place—fourth generation—and is doing a fabulous job.) I knew I could stay—I also knew it would never be "mine."

My in-laws wintered in Mesa, Arizona—snowbirds. When we visited them, I gravitated to the new home sites, still fascinated by the process. The economy had improved—people were buying homes again.

Continental Homes was the largest homebuilder in Arizona—1800 homes a year at that time. Just for giggles, I grabbed an application—also got one for U.S. Home—the largest builder in the country. The applications sat in my desk drawer for six months while I sold farm equipment.

My self-confidence was shot. I knew I was a nobody from Idaho—a hick from the sticks. There'd been thirty-four kids in my high school graduating class and I still considered finishing fifth in the State track meet the one of the biggest accomplishments of my life. And, I had abandoned my brother.

But, something kept niggling at me—maybe just the thoughts of another winter. I filled out the applications and mailed them.

Four months later, Continental Homes finally called and asked me to come in for an interview. I said I would need a couple of weeks, so I could get an airline ticket and get down there. (There was silence on the phone.) "You don't live here?" the marketing manager asked.

"No, if you read my application you will see that I am in Idaho."

"Okay, get here as quickly as you can."

Ecstatic, I bought an airline ticket and went shopping. I thought I should try to fit in. I forgot the Knickerbocker lesson—"the truth." I went a little overboard.

When I arrived, I sat in the foyer for an hour.

"Does the manager know I'm here?"

"Oh yes," she said. *"He knows."*

I should have picked up in the tone.

When I entered the office, I would have sworn the manager modeled for *GQ*. He was fashionably dressed, wearing a crisp, starched, French-cuffed shirt, perfectly knotted tie (with tie bar), double-breasted suit, and shoes that looked like they'd been out of the box for about three minutes.

I don't think he was taken with my white slacks, pink shirt and sockless boat shoes. (I thought they were casual in Arizona—probably should have asked.)

"Do you have your Arizona real estate license?"

"You asked me that on the phone. No, I don't, but I will get one as quickly as possible."

"Glade, we're Continental Homes. We have hundreds of applicants for every position—and most of them are seasoned real estate professionals. If you move here and get your license, feel free to give me a call. I'll try to squeeze you in."

I left. We'd talked for *ten minutes!*

A few months later, caller ID told me I had a call from Dallas. I didn't know anyone there, but I listened to the message. It was U.S Home—headquartered in Dallas.

I called. The gentleman on the other end was very nice.

"Are you still interested in selling homes in Arizona?"

"Very much."

"But, you do not have a real estate license."

"No." I was sure the interview was over.

"Well, that's not a problem. We have a process here. Could you get to Dallas soon?"

He gave me a few dates. I ignored that Laura was expecting our fourth child and took the first one I thought I could make. This time, I did my homework.

A trip to the Library gave me a lot of information. America's leader in home construction was conservative and buttoned down. They expected their consultants to drive a four-door car (to accommodate clients) and to wear a white (not pink) shirt and a tie to work every day.

I bought a blue, pinstriped suit, a new white shirt and a red tie. My brother-in-law took a break from his work as a high-speed photography equipment salesman to companies like General Motors and Morton Thiokol and picked me up. When we landed, Dallas was in full freak-out mode.

It was snowing.

When I called U.S. Home, the interviewer said, "Sir, Dallas doesn't have snow moving equipment. Why don't you come in when the roads are clear?"

I stifled a laugh. "I'm from Idaho. Two inches of snow isn't going to bother me. I'll be there on time if that is okay with you."

They were not interested in either my charisma or sales ability. I took a battery of IQ, personality and aptitude tests. U.S Home had learned that only certain people could handle its culture. They weeded out unsuitable folks early. I looked at shapes, sizes and widgets and answered all manner of odd questions.

I went home without an answer. I had always closed the deal. Despair threatened to sink me.

Another four months slipped by as I sold this combine and that tractor. Fall was approaching when the phone rang. Dallas.

"Are you still interested in the Arizona job?"

"Absolutely."

"We are sorry for the delay. You did very well on the tests. We just had a lot of applicants—a lot. If you can get your license, you can begin on March 15 (1984)."

Packing…new schools…real estate classes… moving—there was a lot to do.

CHAPTER 7
ARIZONA DAWN

To refresh—job offer—we had to sell the house—I needed to enroll in real estate school in Arizona by early December—take the test sometime in January—wait 6-8 weeks to hear that I had, indeed, passed the test—and report to work on March 15 or the job went to someone else.

Oh, and by this time, we had four daughters.

We got the home on the market and I left Laura and the kids for the entire month of December. Yes, I went to Arizona—they got to stay in Idaho. When we didn't get any offers on the house, we decided to pack up, leave and rent the house if we could. Just before we pulled out, I javelined the snow shovel as far as I could into a snow bank.

"Last time I ever pick up one of those," I said.

We arrived in AZ, had Christmas and our listing expired in Idaho on our house. I had ads in the paper for renters.

I got a call from an Idaho agent. "I have a buyer,"

I knew this game. He wanted to list the house. Then, the mystery buyer would "back out."

"No," the agent said. "They are interested but they have to sell a mobile home before they can qualify."

Long story short—we sold the house. I got no equity.

I took a mobile home in trade. It was sitting in a trailer park in Preston, Idaho.

I worked a deal to sell the mobile home and pocketed $11,500 we could use for a new place in Arizona. Now all I had to do was pass the test.

By March 3, I still had not heard. We had been in Arizona for two months. While the economy was better, interest rates were still high. But, houses were selling.

For the life of me I cannot remember exactly when I got the letter, but I passed the test—without a lot of room to spare, calendar-wise. I went to work at U.S. HOME, Phoenix South Division. Sherman Haggerty was my Division President. He was a hard-charging, Dallas native with a reputation for toughness and a very low tolerance for excuses—as in *zero*.

Three or four others started the same day. We got the paperwork settled and went to visit our neighborhoods. The job was 100% commission.

Marilyn, VP of Construction, drove me around. She said, "Well, Glade, they didn't do you any favors."

"What do you mean?"

"Tempe Royal Palms is our slowest moving subdivision. Our highest-priced homes. With interest rates where they are, you may never sell a single house."

Marilyn was a fountain of optimism.

I met my sales partner—Dean Doty—6'3", 350 pounds of Iowa beef. I am 5'8" and 160 if I jump in the pool in my suit and topcoat. We were a pair.

Not sure why, but I called my partner Doan—Doan Deety. We became great friends.

The homes were beautiful. We had the A Plan, B Plan and C plan (the most expensive). South Tempe is a few miles from Arizona State and contained some of the most expensive homes in the area. Many of the homes were custom built—they took a long time, which meant a very slow-arriving commission check.

We had to pre-sell, then get the permits from the city and build from the ground up. Even if I sold a house my first day, it would be three to four months before I got a commission check. And, Marilyn had already told me this subdivision was a bust.

I had a choice—I could listen to Marilyn and accept slow (or no) sales, or I could go to work. Knowing I had four "baby robins" in my nest who were craning their necks for *food,* and understanding I was the sole provider, I chose "Door #2."

I drove Dean nuts those first few months. I wasn't selling anything. I kept asking, "What am I doing wrong?" "Should I change my pitch?" "What should I have said?"

Dean was not exactly rolling, but he was making sales. He'd had time to establish a clientele.

Hope was on the horizon. California was leaking tech companies—and Arizona was catching them. Intel had just announced the building of a plant in Tempe. Arizona State was opening a state-of-the-art research park. Motorola was growing, and other high-tech companies were gravitating to the arid warmth of the Grand Canyon State.

I will never forget a customer from California. He loved the C plan and he was moving here, no doubt about it. He kept talking about the great house he was leaving in California. We loaded up the house just the way he wanted it with lot of extras, a pool, and nice appliances. The price was nearly $190,000. No one had ever sold a house that expensive in Tempe Royal Palms. Interest rates were high, and lenders were using creative financing options where you could adjust your interest rate over three years.

"How much are the payments?" he asked.

I had been in Idaho. I'd never quoted anything over $500.

I took a breath. "$1800."

"Are you serious?" he said. "You have got to be kidding me."

I started Rolodex-ing my mind for excuses.

"Do you know how much this place would cost in Cali? It would be $4,000 a month. I am so moving here!"

We signed everything that afternoon.

Doan Deety and I were killing it. Sherman Haggerty was sure we were up to no good. He sent secret shoppers to check us out—to investigate if we were being honest.

Construction started everywhere on the vacant lots. We were running out of lots to sell and Corporate had not even started to discuss Phase II. We begged Sherman to push. The lots were a bit bigger and more desirable. Phase I was starting to look picked over—the remaining lots were not optimal.

Before long, Sherman let us take reservations for Phase II. The subdivision was on fire and Doan and I had the matches. Soon Tempe Royal Palms was the number one producing community for the Phoenix South Division.

My confidence grew, and I realized that whether you came from Po Dunk Idaho with thirty-four kids in your graduating class or from the big cities of the east, what matters is putting in the work. Control the negative conversations you have in your mind, show up, tell the truth and *bust it*.

I am forever grateful to U.S. Home for believing in me, so I could believe in myself.

CHAPTER 8
THE ELEVATOR GOES BOTH WAYS

After living in Arizona and selling houses for U.S.Home, I decided to try my own business. My father was a great teacher, but not very knowledgeable about business. I am positive he would have taught me whatever he knew—he just didn't know. He really didn't care about money and, to many, business is only about money.

Anyway, what I learned about business I learned on my own—the hard way. You could fit what I knew about owning my own shop into a very small hat. I figured you put up a shingle and you were in business.

Boom—in rolls the money!

Nothing could be further from the truth. I began a home-building company. I got my general contractor's license (not an easy task) and felt I had a very good grasp on the local market. I started advertising and began building houses. Again, because of the dynamics of the Boomers, I didn't have to be very good; I just had to be in the market.

I was doing pretty well until greed entered the picture. (Ever heard this sad tale before?) Well—here it is again, because *everyone* is susceptible. I did not have a business plan, something strategic to lay out growth and expansion. Instead, I began thinking short-term. I wanted more… and I wanted it now.

I fell prey to wanting stuff…and doodads…and "the latest and greatest." I focused on image and pride—and I really wanted everyone to see my success.

I wanted a bigger house, newer vehicle, better neighborhood, and better schools. What I had was pretty crappy and the new stuff was *nice*. I liked what I saw in the showrooms and I wanted it all.

They say hindsight is 20/20 for a reason Looking back, I can see exactly what went wrong and why. Not only did this happen to me at this point, but it would happen again several times. (Stay tuned!)

One of my framing subcontractors approached me with an offer. He would serve as the field supervision of all the homes and free up my time to sell more houses. Our partnership would be a good mix of office and field supervision. He would watch out for our concerns out in the field and I would take care of office controls, selling and such. It sounded like a great idea, and it was for the most part.

We were selling homes as fast as we could build them. We were very visible, and our company's reputation was growing. We were making a mark in our small area and things were going well.

One day my partner told me he was going through some tough times at home. Truth was, he had been sleeping in one of our model homes for a couple of weeks. He was going through a divorce. His personal life was a disaster. And his attention to business details wasn't much better. He was preoccupied with personal matters and was soon spending a lot of his time in, at best, non-business-related activities. He spent a good portion of every day on personal phone calls. I started getting calls from customers.

Things in the field were a mess. Sub-contractors complained about scheduling issues. On top of everything else, the economy slowed. Unbeknownst to anyone, the savings and loan crisis was just around the corner.

Before we could blink, the entire construction environment had changed. Phoenix was the epicenter of the largest savings and loan scandal in history. The business environment turned toxic. Construction money disappeared.

Appraisals took a nosedive. Lenders could not lend. The number one housing market in the country shriveled like a banana peel on hot asphalt. My partner filed for bankruptcy in his framing business and he took off. I could not find him. In one day, our partnership became a sole proprietorship.

We had millions of dollars of debt and a lot of homes we had contractually agreed to build. It was my responsibility to build whatever we could and to satisfy all debts. When the dust settled, I was faced with nearly $400,000.00 of debt.

Memories of leaving my brother bubbled to the surface. Now, I was the one left to clean up the mess. Karma.

Fortunately, I built a home for the President for the Phoenix Division of a large, publicly held homebuilder. Brian knew my situation and believed in my abilities. He asked if I would be V.P. of Operations for the Phoenix Division. I accepted—with one condition—I would have to finish building all of the homes I had under contract.

I told him I would work in the early mornings and late at night for the next six months to finish everything and that I would not let it deter me from what he needed me to do. He agreed.

I finished the homes, sold my personal residence and took whatever money I could spare from the income from my personal salary to pay off the debts. It was difficult on me and my family but I built all those houses and paid off every dime we owed.

This was my first experience with publicly traded companies. I got great experience and insight that would serve me well down the road. Through purchases, mergers and acquisitions, the company became the eighth largest homebuilder in the country. The amalgamation of people, systems, warranties, class action lawsuits as well as other legal issues, storage of documents and many other issues all stemming from merging companies helped me considerably when I went through similar things with Rexall, Enrich and Unicity. Without the valuable information, insight and first-hand experience I gleaned, I am not sure how I would have reacted through those years.

A great many people left Unicity during our recent transition—and I understand.

The issues we faced in Phoenix were formidable. Tremendous changes were in the air; people lost their jobs right and left. One of my responsibilities as V.P of Operations was to downsize the operation. Yes, I had to lay people off—even my personal assistant. Our policy was to give them the news, let them clean out their desk, get the keys and show them the door.

When I told her, she cried—she was hurt.

"What?"

"I don't have a ride."

So, after firing her, I had to give her a ride home.

Not a lot of banter on the way.

We were losing millions—we needed to combine a lot of operations. Property values were sinking like the Lusitania. Over the next two years, we endured a massive reorganization not only in Phoenix, but also in sister cities all over the country. Some operations simply closed.

Of course, I had to have a place for my family to live. We found a beautiful lot in a very nice neighborhood for a bargain. The developer had the same problems as our company; he was selling lots for a huge discount. We began construction of our new dream home, slated to move in for Christmas.

Two weeks before Christmas, the corporate people from Denver came to town. We had worked hard to prepare all the documents and information they requested. When I walked into the President's office, he was not there.

And, I was told my services "would no longer be needed."

Some of the good ole' boys who had been with the company a long time were coming in to take over this lean mean money machine. They had worked for the company in some of the markets that were now closing and Corporate decided to take care of them. My friend and I were expendable.

We had done all the dirty work of downsizing, consolidating, re-tooling and writing down huge losses just for these guys to come in and take all the credit. Not only that, I had a huge bonus coming at the end of the year—one, they informed me, that would not be paid. I did not know how I was going to close on my new house with no job.

When I called Laura, she burst into tears. I had an "aha" moment: Corporate America cares only about the bottom line. People are a commodity—a means to an end. Profitability always trumps individuals.

I do not believe in companies. I believe in people because people are what make companies great.

Somehow, someway, we closed on the house. We moved in and started a new life. I began a construction framing business, subcontracting for home builders. We assembled a host of great people and soon, I was in corporate boardrooms, talking to purchasing agents and operations people—the same thing I had done for several years. I knew what major homebuilders needed and I knew I could provide what was missing.

We quickly grew and had a lot of work. Our little company soon had over 150 employees. That was the good news. The bad news? It took a lot of money to fund payroll every week. Again, my competitiveness, drive to "be bigtime" and my impatience surfaced. I seldom turned down work. I needed capital.

Major homebuilders kept calling me. Why? Because we gave fantastic service and our workers (there's that "people" thing again) were great. I stood behind them and made them feel appreciated. We began hiring Hispanic workers. They could not read blueprints and many of them could not speak English, but they were willing to work as many hours as they could get. I hired a few returned Mormon missionaries who had spent time in Spanish speaking areas. We had lines of communication and fabulous workers. We built a system with English classes for the Hispanic workers and Spanish classes for the Anglo workers—one of the first area companies to implement the concept.

Fifteen years later, Hispanic workers dominate the framing industry, a new generation of bilingual individuals who run the crews and frame the majority of the homes in the Valley of the Sun. All they needed was a chance.

In my Unicity business, I began to focus on the Latino market in the U.S. I knew they would do similar outstanding work in the MLM business. I loved their work ethic. I loved their passion. I loved their loyalty for those individuals who believed in them and were willing to give them a chance. They are great family people. (Whoever came up with the lazy Mexican man sleeping under a palm tree was a monstrous liar.)

But, in my haste to grow, I made another mistake—a bad one. I tried to borrow money for growth, but the nature of our business was such that banks did not like to lend money for payroll. So, I took on a partner.

Fool me once…fool me twice…

I gave him half of my company. One day, two years later, he walked in my office. "I don't trust you anymore," he said. "I want out."

He did not know anything about our business, but he thought he knew everything.

"Set the price and conditions," I said. "I'll decide if I want to buy or sell."

It's a great "break-up" formula. Set the price too low, the other one will buy. Set the price too high, the other will sell.

I sold.

But, I felt really bad for my people because I knew this guy would run the company into the ground. He did.

Within eighteen months, in the middle of a major housing boom in Arizona, he bankrupted the company. Most of the employees went to another company owned by a good friend of mine, who has since treated them all very well. Still, if I had taken my time, I'd still own the company and it would be a multi-million-dollar operation today.

I blew it.

I was right about the trends and the timing of the ventures, but I lacked the wisdom to pace myself.

I didn't know what to do. I had no plan—I had no business—I had no clue.

I'd put my heart and soul into my framing business.

Now, someone else owned it.

I'd blown it twice.

CHAPTER 9
INTRODUCTION TO MLM

Shortly after I had graduated I received a phone call from a friend from my mission days. David told me that he and his wife had something very special they wanted to share with us. They wanted us to come to their home and hear the good news. I tried my best to pry out of him what it was about and to his credit, he would not divulge.

His home was prepared, nicely, and there was a group of about thirty guests. A man began a presentation by drawing circles on a whiteboard. Everyone was thrilled—until he said the name of the company: Amway. The bubble popped.

Some people were upset; others were amused.

This was my introduction to Multi-Level Marketing (MLM). A few years later, I heard the same pitch from another good friend, Blake. He was busting his hump, but not making any money.

I'd run across people in MLM before, but none of them seemed very successful. Some of them had fire in their eyes—they believed in what they were doing—but I never say anyone "making it."

They all followed the same roadmap—instantaneous excitement for six-to-nine months—then the love affair sputtered into nothingness. I understood the concept of geometric growth. I understood the dynamics of the business and I really liked that. However, I never met anyone with what you would call a significant MLM career,

All that changed when Danny White, the former NFL quarterback with the Dallas Cowboys, was hosting a small private gathering at his parents' home in Mesa, Arizona, near where I lived. Some peers invited me to meet Danny to hear about Nu Skin. I must admit, I couldn't have cared less about Nu Skin; I was excited to meet Danny White.

"Sure, I'll attend the meeting," I said. I was a huge sports fan, and this was *Danny White*. As he explained his career and subsequent involvement with Nu Skin, I could not believe he was selling skin creams, lotions and potions. As he was winding down, he called for questions.

I said, "Danny, practically everyone in the U.S. knows who you are; aren't you embarrassed to admit you have sunk so low as to do MLM?"

He was very courteous but now, looking back, he was probably ready to boot me out of his house. He answered, "Well, Glade, I understand why you asked that but if you really understood how big this business is, you wouldn't. Instead, you'd be asking how to get involved."

I figured out a few years later (Idaho farm boy, you know) that he was telling me, with a smile on his face, that I was a little slow and a bit inept. He did it with grace and professionalism, but I would have loved to read the words within the little cloud above his head. Over the course of about three months, I met with those who had invited me, and they tried to educate this old Idaho plow pusher.

Many nights we would be in the Casita office of John McClellan until 1 or 2 A.M. They must have printed three dozen spreadsheets with every possible scenario. Slowly, I began to grasp the concept. Eventually, I signed up.

I am so grateful for the time spent as a Nu Skin distributor. I was fortunate to work side-by-side with many of the company's top distributors.

Nathan Ricks is a giant in the industry—one of the all-time, most successful builders in the MLM world. He also created staggering wealth as a real estate mogul. I worked side-by-side with Nathan, receiving invaluable teaching and coaching at his feet while traveling to many countries in Asia.

What a legend!

These people have earned and continue to earn hundreds of dollars in override commissions for the time and effort they spent in their early days at Nu Skin. These people are true professionals and my time with them shaped many of my views, opinions and global perspectives. How grateful I am to them for their teaching and, more importantly the systems, concepts and fundamentals they taught—fundamentals, concepts and systems that are endemic to all of MLM, regardless of the company.

I saw the size of their checks. I saw the cars they drove. I saw the lifestyles they lived. These were my neighbors and I knew who they were and what they had accomplished. They were not a bunch of unemployed, pocket protector, Sansabelt slack-wearing people. These were people with options. These were people who owned companies and sold them in order to do this business.

During my construction career, my income was 100% dependent upon the local economy. If the local economy was doing well, I prospered. If the local economy was doing poorly or if interest rates were bad, I suffered. In other words, my income was contingent on variables out of my control and confined to a relatively close proximity to where I lived. These Nu Skin guys were talking about a *global opportunity* without geographic boundaries and a business opportunity that transcends traditional business. There are no growth restrictions. If one excels and is willing to pay the price, work hard and catch the vision of this financial vehicle, he/she can be as big as he/she wants. It is completely possible to grow a multi-national, global business. I really liked that idea.

So, I went to work and traveled to Taiwan, Hong Kong, Japan, New Zealand and Australia. I witnessed the unfolding of Nu Skin in these countries. The excitement and the vision became crystal clear to me. For some, it truly had become a global business. Those who had the vision were earning income from every precinct in Japan, every corner of Taiwan and from every state and practically every berg in the USA. I knew it was true and I wanted a piece of it. I worked part-time building my Nu Skin business at the same time I was building my framing company. I worked diligently at it for nearly two years until I realized that perhaps I was too late. Although I had stepped to the compensation pinnacle—Diamond Status—the people I recruited were not enjoying similar success. I began to question many things and I felt better when I backed off Nu Skin and focused on my construction company.

As I was building my construction company, which later I sold, I could not get the experience of Nu Skin out of my mind. I loved MLM. I loved the positive people. I loved the ability to travel and meet new people from around the world. I loved the passion of people trying to better their station in life. I loved hearing about people's having success with the products.

MLM was in my veins and I liked it. With the experience of Nu Skin fresh in my mind, I looked for nearly four years (investigating about forty companies) before I found Rexall. I signed up as a Rexall Independent Business Owner in late 1995 or early 1996 but I didn't do much with it. I liked everything about it, but I asked the question, "What about International?"

I wanted to "go big or go home," but Rexall was not ready.

CHAPTER 10
THE WORST FINANCIAL MISTAKE OF MY LIFE

After I had sold my framing company, I had time on my hands. I had some money and so my wife and I took our four daughters to Australia for a month. We had a terrific experience.

Soon after returning home, Brian called me. He'd just moved to Salt Lake City, Utah to head up another publicly traded company's division. He needed a framing company. Salt Lake City was beginning to transform from a mom and pop-type place to a market for big builders.

The city had never had production framing operations like the one I owned in Phoenix and my friend wanted to work with pros.

After a month or so of deliberation, Laura and I decided to give it a shot. Finding skilled carpenters presented a challenge. Every time I tried to introduce a new concept, I heard, "Not how we do it here in Utah!"

Fortunately, things were slowing down in the California market. A considerable number of Hispanic workers were traveling the country looking for employment. I met up with Javier Rodriguez; we clicked immediately. We recruited several dozen Hispanic carpenters and were soon dominating the Salt Lake market. No one had ever seen an operation like ours.

In six months, our company was buying more lumber and framing more houses than anyone else in the entire state. But, there was a problem.

While everyone loved the product, they did not love the prices. They wanted to pay what they had paid mom and pop. We couldn't make that work.

I bet you think I'd learned my lesson—think again. Trying to be the big dog, I'd grown too fast and taken on too much overhead. I did everything I could think of to get the builders to pay more. I wanted to hire skilled people and to pay them what they were worth. We had three forklifts and every site had a superintendent who ensured timeliness and production quality.

In my haste to succeed, I had not listened to warnings. I worked with a particular builder despite the fact others had cautioned me about his practices. His company ended up owing me a lot of money. He "slow paid" me. That made it tough for me to pay my guys.

I fell behind in my accounts payable—suppliers started to call. I sometimes used money earmarked for suppliers to pay my workers—it's not good business, I know. But, I wanted to take care of the people who were working for me.

I should have tried out for the circus—I was a master juggler. The suppliers were after me, and I was pressuring the builder. It worked for a while. But, even the best "thrower and catcher" eventually drops a plate.

The suppliers did not care if I paid my guys—they wanted their money, which is understandable. They wouldn't work with me, but either I'd lost my silver-tongued touch, or they'd been burned too often. Almost every day, the sheriff delivered another summons. The kids recoiled at first, but eventually got to the point where they would look through the blinds and shout, "Dad, the sheriff's here again."

I shut it down and had to declare personal bankruptcy. In my mind, only the most inept, scandalous people filed for bankruptcy.

It was an embarrassing and dark time. My self-esteem was shot.

No income.

But, the kids still needed lunch money…and clothes…and supplies…and…and…and…

I wanted to turn back to MLM.

I knew it wasn't a quick fix. Building a network takes time. Almost every business has a three-year curve. If you can break even after 36 months, you are a success. I didn't have that long.

Knowing MLM takes time, I sent my construction resume out to every headhunter from New York to San Francisco in hopes of getting a J.O.B. I needed to provide for my family. The phone did not ring once. I could not believe it, so I started calling.

One said, "You don't have enough experience."

The next one, "You have too much experience."

Another one, "You're too specialized."

What I heard—bottom line—no candy coating—"Glade, you stink!"

I kicked myself every day—every hour—every minute—a lot of "stinkin' thinkin'" and negative self-talk.

To make ends meet, I sold everything I could find—ladders, extension cords, saws, nail guns—anything to keep food on the table and to keep the family from panic.

In eighteen months, we did the ole' "penthouse to the outhouse" routine. I could not believe I had been so foolish—and foolhardy. I could see the disappointment in the kids' eyes. For nearly twenty years, we'd been in great shape.

Not anymore.

I was cold and rude to Laura. Our credit rating went down the drain, a hit that plagued us for many years.

I kept dreaming of a global business. I knew the potential was there. I just had to find the opening.

Then, I get a call. It was Randy.

"There's a chance to expand into Asia," he said. "And, you are the man to do it."

My golden opportunity—the largest consumer market in the world.

And I was broke.

CHAPTER 11
HOPE RISES IN THE EAST

In February of 1997, the Direct Sellers Association (DSA) reported the largest market in the world (47% of consumers) was Asia—not counting the 1.3 billion folks in China. Within Asia, Japan ranked the number one market in the world. I believe the numbers are very similar today.

I wanted to be the one who introduced Rexall Showcase International that market place. There was only one problem? It was expensive to travel over to and around Asia. I had a great company—great products—a great market—fabulous timing—a huge potential upside—knowledge—and experience.

I did not have money.

I called Terry. We'd worked together at NuSkin. Though his situation was not as dire as mine, he was in a difficult position and he had some business connections in Japan. We sent out an email blast to as many Japanese contacts as we could find. (We had to use dial-up mode, by the way.) We worked late into the night putting together the communication.

I awakened the next day and raced to the computer to check on the responses.

"Your AOL account has been suspended for lack of payment."

What a kick in the stomach. Anyone who might have replied would have received a "Returned Email" notice.

I called AOL. They were polite and listened intently. They were more than happy to restore my account—as soon as I paid $67.

I had $5 to my name. Terry did not have much more.

I went to the garage and got my last two nail guns—original price, $350 each. The pawn shop offered me $35 apiece. I paid AOL (leaving me with $3) only to discover I had not received a single reply. (Never did reclaim those nail guns.) Terry and I put a business plan together and started looking for an investor. We assembled all the data we could about direct sales, Japan, Asia and our NuSkin experience. We assured everyone with whom we met that we were going to set sales records like the world had never previously seen. We had income projections and charts and graphs.

It was awesome.

Terry approached several of his former investors in real estate. I headed to my colleagues in the construction and development arenas. We offered a percentage of income (for a limited time) or a fairly high interest rate. We weren't looking for a lot of money, but some of the folks we saw could not have reinstated my AOL account.

Everybody was hurting—or not interested. Everybody passed on what they assured us sounded like a "great opportunity."

One guy reached in his pocket and handed me two dollars. "Here, Glade," he said, "if you have some vitamins or something else for sale for this price, drop them buy next time you come. Good luck."

I was very close to hanging out on the corner with a "Will Work for Food" sign, but this was insulting.

I said, "I am desperate for someone to believe in me, but I am not desperate enough to take hand-outs. Thank you for your thoughtfulness," and walked out of his office.

I went to see Bob. We'd worked together right out of Utah State. I explained my situation to him and two others.

After I'd run through the pitch, he said, "You didn't have to drive the twelve hours. Why didn't you just call? I'm happy to help."

He excused his colleagues. When they were gone, he said, "Buddy, I know you're desperate and I have some misgivings about this, but you obviously need someone to believe in you. I don't need to make any money off this. I've been blessed. I've always liked you—and I think you are going to make this work, if anyone can."

Bob helped me as a humanitarian gesture.

I am forever grateful.

But I did pay him back plus an incredible return on his investment.

***

I headed to Japan and Hong Kong in search of some associates. This was the toughest "sale" of my lifetime. Let's look at my bullet points.

Here's what I said:

- U.S. company with a long history and brand recognition
- Asia is the greatest market in the world for our industry
- Products deal with health issues of aging population
- You could be the first to bring this company and these products to Asia
- There will be challenges but it will be worth it

Here is what they thought:

- So, the company does not yet have an office in this country and the products are not registered with the Ministry of Health. Are they safe and is it legal to import the products without such approval?

- How do we know these products work with Asian people? Do you have any case studies of Asian people using these products?

- Do you have any material in Japanese or Chinese?

- How do I get paid? How do I register my people? Who takes care of the genealogy and where do my checks go?

- How do I know that the company will in fact open an office here some day?

Silly me. I was expecting people half a world away to dive into our company based on my word alone. I outlined the protocol. They would register as US distributors on US registration forms. They would be considered US distributors. They would all be registered to my home address and all checks would be in US dollars and sent to my home in Arizona. Upon receipt of any check we would send the money to the appropriate individual in Japan or Hong Kong. They would deposit the check in their bank and wait nearly one month for it to clear and post to their account.

Furthermore, our company would not ship to them in Japan or Hong Kong. All orders had to come via fax. Then we would get on the phone and order the products, pay sales tax to the state of Arizona, pay domestic shipping to Arizona. We would re-package the products and ship them internationally to Japan and Hong Kong.

The entire process was tedious, laborious, slow and costly. I recall boxing up the very first orders, filling out all the customs forms and taking them down to my friend Marilyn's. She owned the "Mail Boxes, Etc." franchise. I had no idea what to expect. Would they go through customs? How long would it take? Would there be duties charged on the Japan side? What condition would the products be in after arrival?

Suffice it to say there was an expensive and frustrating learning curve on both sides of the Pacific. Orders kept coming and the business started to grow. Remember, both Terry and I were in dire financial conditions. We soon recognized the need for a shipping operation. We explored many options, but our credit was too poor to establish an account with Federal Express or UPS. Terry had an acquaintance who had a small warehouse operation with a little space.

More importantly, Robert and Kate (father and daughter) had good credit. They were open to the idea. We could not pay them anything, so Terry arranged to sponsor the Bowens and placed the Japan organization, downline of the Bowens. The connection would be their pay. Theoretically the shipping would pay for itself and help them build their group in Japan.

The Bowen family was fantastic! We could not have done what we did without them. Kate's organizational skills in the office and Bob's tireless efforts in the warehouse (Terry and I handled the phones) worked beyond my wildest dreams. We processed orders, received them, re-boxed everything, filled out customs forms, collaborated with Japan distributors, solved problems and did everything else necessary to facilitate more than $2,000,000 a month worth of orders before the company officially opened in Japan. The Bowens were a godsend.

We learned that the Japan Government would allow a certain number of products, for personal use only, to come to each household per month. This knowledge jumpstarted the beginning of the NFR (not for resale) operations that many MLM companies use to this day in many parts of the world. We cracked the code!

Companies began to "place" people inside our organization in Japan to learn our process. In fact, the acting Co-CEO and Co-Owner of our company, Unicity International, told me that when he was V.P. of International Sales for Enrich International, they did that very thing. They had people join our group in Japan to learn how we were getting so many products into Japan without registering with the Ministry of Health.

Enrich International began a company sponsored NFR Program.

Enrich International hired Japanese-speaking customer service people, translated materials into Japanese, did not charge sales tax and began shipping directly from the corporate facilities, thereby eliminating domestic shipping charges as well as state sales taxes. I'd asked Dave Schofield (CEO of Rexall Showcase International) to do the exact same thing. He said "no."

Consequently, Enrich International soon had a sales volume in Japan six-times larger than RSI's.

Expenses still outran income. Remember, Bob had to loan me money—and some of that fed my family. As time went on, I realized, despite his gracious assistance, I had not asked for enough money.

Have you ever been to Tokyo? If you stay in a hotel, a Coke or a coffee will run you about $10. A decent room is a minimum of $200. Something like the Hyatt tips out at $500 a night.

I was presenting a "once in a generation—once in a lifetime—opportunity." I couldn't meet potential participants at the Motel 6. I had to portray success. So, we would meet at the Hilton. I didn't say I *stayed* at the Hilton. I'd bed down someplace a lot less expensive but within walking distance. Then, I would keep appointments at the swankier place.

When my colleagues said they'd be bringing six or seven to meet me, the business part of me was happy. The more practical side was counting heads and thinking, "Geez, there goes another couple of hundred in drinks." I had not anticipated such cumbersome expenses when I was "begging at Bob's."

The money soon ran out. In Hong Kong, Randy had rented a small meeting room on the Kowloon side of Hong Kong. We kept some inventory there and had the capacity to host about a hundred folks. We did one-on-one meetings during the day and larger events in the evenings. I always walked the last guests out.

In Hong Kong, from midnight to 2 AM is noodle time. These people never sleep! It is customary for them to be out until the wee hours of the morning having noodles or drinking.

When they invited me, I always came up with an excuse. "Oh, I am sorry, I must call back to the US right now, so you guys run ahead and if I end the call soon enough, I will join you." I simply could not afford to join them. Little did they know that I stored a small foam pad with two large beach towels and a pillow in the meeting room. I slept there whenever I could.

Good cost. The amenities—not so hot!

The office had a key pad security system. Most of the distributors knew the code. I was constantly afraid someone would come into the office early in the morning and see me sleeping on the floor with my foam pad and two towels. Therefore, I awakened very early in the morning.

Ah—the glamorous life of the American Financial Guru.

Since there was no shower in the office, I walked across the street to the public swimming pool where I would shave, shower and get myself ready for the day. The water in the shower would back up over my ankles. I tried not to think about what I was wading in. But, at least I was clean and prepared to tell my appointments, "Hey, stay with this and you can be rich, just like me."

Those were character building times. In July of 1997, Laura, my wife of twenty years and the mother of our four daughters, asked me for a divorce. The business was just barely beginning to show a pulse; we were on the right track, but she could not take the roller coaster any more.

We are all products of our environments. Her father was a second-generation business executive—very successful. My dear father could not tell business from a bass fiddle. She'd grown up with security and certainty. I thought everyone struggled—worried about the weather—understand that if it did not rain at the right time, there would be scarcity. I did not like watching my enterprises go belly-up, but I'd seen failure before and I knew I could start something else.

To be very clear here, we were not a good fit. Still, I take full responsibility for the break-up. Laura told me that since I started the dream of having a successful MLM business, our relationship had worsened. She told me to give up and get a real job. She still wanted a divorce, but she counseled me to return to the life of a salesperson where I had created more stability.

Now I was broke and a failure as a husband. The divorce was finalized in January of 1998. I take a lot of the responsibility for the failed marriage. To this day, things are very amicable between my ex-wife and me. When we split, I told her to determine what she needed financially, and I would pay. Occasionally we would have spats over this or that and both of us would say things in front of the children that we should not have, but for the most part, the situation has been without hostility. In fact, years later after I had remarried, Laura invited her sisters, her mother and Cindy (my new wife) to a cooking class as a Christmas present.

"One big happy family!" ☺

CHAPTER 12
THINGS ARE LOOKING UP

By early spring of 1998, our business in Japan had exploded. Sales were nearing $400,000 a month and my income was over $15,000.00 a month. Expenses were still quite high as a result of working in, flying to and moving around Japan, Hong Kong and now, Taiwan. I was divorced with no real place to stay when I got home from traveling in Asia. I had no personal relationships because I would never stay in one place long enough to establish one.

In short, I was lonely and homeless.

Laura's father, Kay, called and asked if I would like to stay at his winter home in Arizona. I could pay him when I got some money.

I accepted his offer and stayed in his double wide mobile home in Mesa, Arizona while I was in the States.

I was usually home near the end of the month to help the Bowens with receiving, repackaging and shipping. Somewhere in the second week of every month Terry and I would take off again.

The Hong Kong section officially opened in November of 1997, which helped some with the shipment of products from Arizona. Still, most of the products were headed to Japan, where we did not officially open a fully-staffed distribution office until May of 1999.

On April 4, 1998, my personal life was at an all-time low. I was a mess. The only thing more compelling than my loneliness was my despair. Although my income was stepping up—I was getting five-digit, monthly checks with regularity—I was miserable.

Being in a different city—a different country—every day may sound glamorous, but it is exhausting and debilitating. I had acquaintances, people with whom I could have dinner and a drink (or a few more), and I could glad-hand my way through almost any metropolis in the world.

But, I did not have any friends on the road.

The few times I tried to date had been disasters. Small talk wasn't my thing. I could sell a product, but when I tried to sell myself, I came across as cheesy—or worse, creepy.

I was in Arizona and had spent a long evening at the warehouse getting all my ducks in a row. And I had been drinking.

On the way home, I heard a pop! I'd driven into the curb and blown out both tires on the right side. I did not realize until much later how fortunate I was not to have struck another vehicle or a pedestrian. But, I was not thinking very clearly during that period—and I certainly wasn't concerned with anyone other than Glade.

Not even the most pessimistic person in the world carries *two* spares. I got my bearings—a little—and limped back to the doublewide on the rims. If an officer had stopped me, a judge would have put me under the jail—and rightfully so.

When I awoke the next day, as the headache diminished, and my vision cleared, I vowed to make some changes. Terry met me, and we headed for the Outback Steakhouse.

"I'm going to help you sharpen your game," he said.

"Huh?" I told you I wasn't doing well.

"Your game. You need to start dating, so you need to know how to talk to women."

I wasn't very interested, but Terry's a good salesman, so we practiced on the bartender. Eventually, Terry left me and went home. The bartender, who'd been very patient, finally said, "Sir, I'm married."

"Who's not?" I asked.

"It's Monday," she said. "We're light on staff. You're on your own."

I looked around and saw a young woman who had a spring in her step. She was moving from table to table faster than any of her cohorts. I nodded towards her and asked the bartender, "Is she involved with anyone?"

"She's going through a divorce. Probably not interested."

"Would you ask her to drop by over here when you get a chance?" I realized I might be coming across a little creepy. "I just want to say hi."

Bonnie, the bartender passed the word.

Nothing happened.

More than a little time passed. I am generally patient, but something was pushing me. "Bonnie," I said, "I promise I'm a good guy. Would you make sure that young woman knows I'm not leaving here until she speaks to me at least once? I don't want to interrupt her while she's working. I'll wait until closing if I have to."

Only later did I learn the waitress was checking me out through a network of strategically-placed spies.

After another considerable wait, she came over.

"My name's Cindy. You need me for something?"

I'd never met a more charming person in my life. We clicked instantly. From that moment, we saw each other every day until I was to leave on Sunday for Asia. We even had a picnic—something I had not done in… well…ever.

It was the most fantastic week of my life.

One night we talked on the phone from 11 PM until 4 AM. Things were moving quickly.

When we said goodbye on Sunday, I gave her my voicemail number where she could leave messages. I promised to call from Tokyo.

Cindy was all I thought about on the flight west. Several days passed without a word. I was confused. Had I imagined everything? Had I been mistaken? Was this a case of out of sight, out of mind?

I waited as many days as I could, then called. I got her niece. She gave me Cindy's schedule. I calculated the time difference. It would be 3 AM in Tokyo, but I would call.

When I heard her voice, fear and doubt launched a dual attack on my heart the second she said hello.

I can't remember if we exchanged pleasantries, but I know I got to the heart of the matter PDQ—"Why haven't I heard from you?"

Cindy burst into tears. "I tried over a hundred times, but kept getting some other company. I figured you had just lied to me."

We checked the number. I had given her the wrong one.

I was as happy as I had ever been to that point in my life. We talked for a long time. I was in Tokyo in a nice hotel room I could actually afford, and she was thousands of miles away in Arizona, but it felt like we were sitting side by side.

We were married on September 9, 1999. I chose the date because I knew even I would remember it—9/9/99.

CHAPTER 13
THE DARKNESS

I was no longer Glade Poulsen

I was Inmate 11550.

11550 received an ID, a wash cloth, a toothbrush, toothpaste and a bar of soap.

I was in Hong Kong. The trip had been scheduled for a day-and-a-half. I knew the city—knew where to go—knew where to avoid. I even knew where to get Mexican food. It's not very often that you get chips and salsa in Asia.

I also knew where to get a drink. I've mentioned my religious background and we are admonished to stay away from alcohol. However, I was not observant of the code of conduct.

It all began to change during my divorce and in the early years of my marriage to Cindy. I'm a Type A personality. At least, that's my excuse. I am probably an alcoholic. I didn't drink all the time, but when I started, I did not stop.

I closed the place along with a group of the migrant workers and nannies who work for the locals. Every Saturday at 6 PM, they are summarily ushered out of the homes where they work and expected to fend for themselves until 9 AM on Monday.

They lived and slept in the parks, under the overpasses, in streets and alleys—anywhere they could find shelter from the seasonal rains or blistering heat.

Here's where the rationalization starts. When I was a boy, Dad hired migrant workers to help "thin" the beets. If the plants grow too close together, they choke out, so once they begin to germinate, farmers (and their help) thin the crop to allow six-to-eight inches between each plant. Navajo men and women gravitated to the work—I don't know why—but they were good at it. They would arrive and live in an old caboose—yes, the train type—as many as twenty or so per car. Back then, we called the male workers "bucks"—in truth, the term is racist and recalls the days of slavery in the South. But I didn't know any better and I like to believe I didn't mean any harm. I thought it was a term of affection.

I was a kid—what did I know?

I want to be perfectly clear here—my father did not tolerate discrimination. He talked to us all the time about the dignity of all people. And, I like to think I have practiced what I learned.

Anyway, a great many of the "bucks" drank—a lot. When Dad paid them at the end of the week, he knew a lot of the money would turn "liquid" if the men were unsupervised. My father would take the men home, then accompany the wives (with the pay money) to the grocery to ensure the family got something to eat.

After that, the men could take whatever allowance they received at home and pass the night at whatever watering hole they fancied.

What does any of this have to do with my night on the town? In Hong Kong, on that fateful evening, I kept buying drinks for a group of ladies—all of them house servants who I knew had been "invited to leave" their places of employment until Monday. Kind-hearted and compassionate to the end (and hammered beyond any ability either to make a rational decision or to foresee trouble), I suggested my room was big enough and had enough bedding for them to come along and stay for the night.

I did not have anything nefarious on my mind. And no sexual activity took place—at least, none I remember. And there was the problem. The next thing I knew, police officers were rousting me from a deep sleep. Bewildered and still drunk, I did not know what to do. Officers rummaged through my stuff and took pictures. Hotel employees stood at the door.

The questions kept coming.

"Where were you last night?"

"Did you invite anyone back to your room?"

"How many came with you?"

"What do you remember?"

I had a vague recollection of hearing noise and awakening to find two of the women going through my wallet. Other than that snippet, however, the previous evening was a blank.

"We're going downtown," one of the cops said.

"For what?" I asked.

The only answer I got was, "We have to go now."

Someone handed me a black bag.

"What's this?"

"A hood for your head."

"Why the hell do I need a hood?"

"There are photographers outside. You do not want your picture in the paper."

I refused to put it on, so they took me out the back in as discreet a fashion as possible.

Before we entered the elevator, they handcuffed me and took me downtown.

The cell was cinder block—a small cement bench in one corner, a hole in the floor for the toilet.

Several hours of torturous memory searching later, an English-speaking officer began questioning me through the bars of my cell.

He went away, and I was alone again for several more hours.

And always the same questions—with one significant addition.

"Did you have sex with any of those women?"

Not being able to remember is a scary thing—and I couldn't. You see, most of the time when I "tied one on," I didn't pass out—I blacked out. It's a common superpower among people with alcohol issues. While everyone else is falling over and going to sleep on the couch, we continue to function; we just can't remember anything.

I kept hearing my Dad. "If you always tell the truth, you'll never forget what you said." So, I did,

All you folks who watch cop shows on television are screaming, "Why didn't you shut up and demand a lawyer?

Truthfully, because: a) I was sure I had not done anything illegal; and, b) I'm a salesman—I knew I could talk my way out of anything.

So, when I got the question, "Did you have sex with any of the women," I answered truthfully.

"I do not know."

My entire experience with the legal system was a traffic ticket in Idaho. I figured if I didn't have anything to hide, I did not need a lawyer—although I asked several times if I should call one. No one ever said "yes," so I went along with the routine.

I figured out how much trouble I was in when someone came in and asked for a DNA sample. I declined—less out of fear for what they would find and more because I was terrified of being stuck by a needle in a Hong Kong jail cell.

An hour later, the Chief of Police came to my cell and informed me I was being charged.

I called my friend and associate Albert. He came immediately.

I told him the entire story—everything I could remember.

The next day, the only attorney I knew in Hong Kong came to see me. He did real estate law, but he got me through the arraignment where I pled "not guilty." Fortunately, the proceedings were conducted in English.

The prosecutor asked for four-to-six weeks for trial prep. My attorney rose. "Your honor, you cannot expect my client to sit in jail for four weeks. We request a bail hearing."

The prosecutor was on her feet. "This is a foreign national, your honor. He has no ties to the community. He has resources. He will flee the jurisdiction."

"Mr. Poulsen will surrender his passport," my attorney said.

Then, to me, he said, "Is that okay?"

I nodded.

The judge ordered a bail hearing in two days.

"You have to stay in jail until the hearing," my attorney said. "Meanwhile, we will get you more appropriate counsel."

I met my new attorney—Samuel.

"You will need $20,000 for your bail and a retainer," he said. "And, you need to know, this case could cost you close to $50,000."

All I could think of was, "Whatever it takes."

Fortunately, I had some assets.

Handcuffed again, I left the courthouse in the back of a truck with about twelve others. I had an irrational fear someone would see me in the paddy wagon—that was the least of my issues.

The handcuffs were tight and every turn or bump ground them into my wrists.

Eventually, we arrived at my new home. LCK PRISON.

My God, I was in prison—not jail—not the county drunk tank—prison.

We stripped, showered, passed through a metal detector and underwent a cavity search. The intake process took six hours.

That's when I lost my name.

That's when I became 11550.

CHAPTER 14
THE BOTTOM OF THE PIT

Someone was yelling. "11550!"

I raised my hand—tentatively.

"Do you want to be in General Group or do you want to be with a special group so as not to have any trouble?"

What does that even mean?

"Quickly," he said. "Which?"

I said, "General Group"

At 6 PM, we marched through a number of barred gates into the middle of the prison. Dinnertime.

Some rice—beans—and a piece of toast.

Then, we went to our cells. Three of us occupied a fifteen square foot box—and part of the space was devoted to the flush-to-the-ground squatter and a sink. During intake, one guy kept staring at me. He looked particularly vile.

Oh yes, he was my "cellie."

He was from Pakistan. The other guy was from India.

Both of them claimed to be victims of a "frame." But I felt the same way, so we have something in common.

The reality of being in this place for the next four days began to sink in. *I could be dead by then.* My stomach began to spasm.

I didn't sleep much that night.

At 6:30 AM, the siren screamed us into consciousness. A recorded message blared through speakers, "It is 0630. Prisoners arise for inspection." A guard went past the cells kicking a five-gallon bucket of tea. I decided to try levity.

"Look," I said, "Room service with no extra charge."

No one laughed.

I shut up. A guard came to the door. "11550, come with me."

We went into an office marked "Head of Security." I waited outside the office for two hours. I had listened to my cellmates' tales of woe and conspiracy all evening. My mouth filled with cotton.

The Head of Security spoke English with a British accent. "I have reviewed your case, read your file and watched you, Mr. Poulsen," he said. "I am concerned for you. You seem like nice fellow."

I started to protest my innocence. He held up his hand.

"I do not care what happened to you out there," he said. "My only concern is what happens to you in here. Would you consider moving to what we call "the Day Room?"

He paused for my answer.

"What is it?" I asked.

"It is a room where you are free to move about during the day; there are ping pong tables, a library and televisions. We put offenders in there for safety reasons. I fear someone may attack or harm you because of your alleged crime. You will be safer in the day room. In the evening, you will be in a cell but for most of your waking hours, you would be in the Day Room. There are only about thirty in there at a time—mostly higher-class individuals who, like you, have no previous record of offense—like you—only most are trade and fraud cases."

Of course, I said yes and was transferred to the Day Room.

So far, Cindy was unaware of my situation. I figured I would be out in no time and no one would be the wiser. Three days later (or was it five—I lost track), I asked Albert to call her.

My first morning in the Day Room, I had written Cindy a letter. Now, I called the American Consulate and asked for a meeting. Hopefully, someone could fax the letter to her. (Eventually, a very nice woman at the Consulate got the letter through.) In the letter, I told Cindy not to come to Hong Kong until after the bail hearing. No reason for her to get there so we could have fifteen minutes through the plexiglass.

I said some other things, too—how much I loved her—an apology for my bad habits (she'd seen the "drinking me")—and I promised big changes. In what I later realized was a significantly tangential issue, I asked her to find out if Kathy had made Triple Diamond status. Business concerns gradually became much less important (the possibility of *years* in prison helps put things in perspective), but at that moment, I still wanted to be Mr. Bigshot Business Guy—I had to look out for my people.

Thursday, I was granted bail at the hearing. I was free to move about Hong Kong. I listened to my attorney's admonition not to leave the country, but I could not have gone even if I wanted. They took my passport.

Cindy came in on Friday. Albert had arranged a hotel for us until I could find better accommodations. As part of my bail agreement, I have to check into the police station three times a week—Monday, Wednesday and Friday—between 1 and 5:00 PM.

Cindy and I could not let go of each other. We hugged and cried. The room had twin beds. We didn't care. We curled up in a bed for one and held each other throughout the night.

***

"My experience is that these cases drag out for a long time."

I looked at Samuel. "How long? Eight weeks?"

"More like nine months," he said. "And that is until the beginning of the trial."

I shook my head. "If we lose, what am I looking at?"

"Minimum seven years—probably something more in the range of fifteen." He said it like he was telling me the bus schedule.

The elation of the airport turned into near-despair. It took a while for me to absorb everything. The hayseed from Idaho was neck deep in fertilizer and no amount of salesmanship, good looks or money was going to get me out of trouble any time soon.

I checked into the Silverline Beach Hotel on the island of Mui Wo. I had a decent room with a shared kitchen at the end of the hall. It was a quiet place—off the beaten path—but still, technically, in Hong Kong.

The room was $800 a month. I needed a twenty-minute ferry ride to get to the police station for check-in. The ferry ran from 6 AM to 9 PM. The lease was month-to-month.

The trial was constantly delayed. On at least four different occasions, we thought we were headed to trial only to have our hopes smashed. Samuel and I would get all geared up, then encounter some glitch—an attorney's vacation—a travel issue—a tardy lab report. My case kept sliding lower and lower—later and later—on the docket.

I could not travel, but I was able to conduct my business over the phone and by email. Cindy and the kids/grandkids were an ocean away. She came to Hong Kong every four-to-six weeks, but it was grueling for her.

As terrible as my situation was, I knew I was fortunate to be in the MLM world. Most people would have lost their income stream. Since

I was part of a larger organization and I had residual income. I was grateful that my income remained steady.

But, my emotions didn't. I kept trying to imagine seven years in prison—fifteen years. I thought about the children I would not see—the graduations I would not attend. Our oldest daughter Kirsten was engaged. I would miss the wedding.

Cindy was constantly talking me off the emotional ledge.

I was alone—mostly—on an island—beating myself up for whatever I had or had not done. At the very least, I had not protected myself. I had put myself in harm's way.

I had not been true to the principles I'd learned as a child—or the ethics I practiced in Denmark. I was angry…I was depressed.

I was suicidal.

Five months into the nightmare, I hit bottom. I had checked into the station. But I missed the last ferry to Mui Wo—I was only two minutes late, but the damn thing sailed without me. I had not seen Cindy for weeks.

I sat on the rocks surrounding the pier. I have no idea what time the sun slipped away, because all I saw was darkness…the gloominess of my situation…the impermeable misery in my heart…the smooth blackness of the water.

I could just start swimming. Eventually, I would run out of steam and sink into the murky bay. The idea didn't seem crazy—it seemed…peaceful.

I heard a voice…*Do it…Do it…Do it.*

I called Cindy. I was going to beg her forgiveness and say goodbye. *Do it…Do it…Do it.*

She deserved better…a better life…a better situation…a better man. *Do it…Do it…Do it.*

I sat on those stupid rocks and wept like I was never going to stop.

Cindy was in tears on the other end, but she kept encouraging me.

"We've got this, baby," she said. "You don't want your children and grandchildren to remember you this way. We have each other. We're going to be fine."

I kept blubbering about the end…and how much better off she'd be…and all sorts of other lunacy. But she never wavered.

And, she finally broke through.

We talked until light shimmered in the East, the sun's rays peaking over the tops of the volcanos as if checking to see if it was safe to come out. When the first ferry of the morning pulled away towards Mui Wo, I was on it.

I slept for the next twenty-four hours.

CHAPTER 15
CLAWING BACK UP

I began flooding my mind by reading everything I could find about positivity—self-help books—autobiographies—anything to return my fighting spirit. Cindy and I decided to send our children over, two at a time, to spend time with me. I set up a conference call with my siblings and told them I was in Hong Kong for an extended period of time because of some trouble but that I had faith and hope I would soon be able to come home. I asked them to trust me and to pray for me. I discussed my plight with my faith's local leadership and sought their help.

Bottom line—I faced my demons and retrained myself about mental toughness and a positive outlook. I remembered all my challenges—losing jobs, divorce and dealing with debt. I relived every valuable lesson I had learned.

The magnificence of the Grand Canyon came about through storms, floods, and blistering heat. I could do this—I would be stronger for it—and I would be better equipped to help other people.

No such word as can't.

The island of Mui Wo featured a steep mountain into which are carved thousands of steps leading to a shrine at the top. On the other side, the mountain descends into Discovery Bay. I made it part of my daily routine to walk up the mountain. It was arduous. At first, I could only manage a fraction of the stairs. Eventually, I jogged up the hillside.

Delays delayed…and continuances continued, but I was getting stronger every day mentally and physically. The dopamine was flowing as were my creative juices. I could have dodged this—probably. Telling the truth drove me head-first into trouble. But I needed this test—I needed the refining fire of adversity—I needed the pressure of the moment. I did not need to be reshaped.

I needed to be reborn!

The trial date arrived. Seven jurors—four men—three women.

It was the British style court room. Barristers wore robes and wigs. I stood in the bullpen in the back of the courtroom where every eye could see me. The prosecutor presented the case and painted a disparaging and awful picture.

Had I been on the jury at that point, I would have convicted myself.

At the end of the third day, after all the other witnesses and reports, a young woman from the Philippines (one of the people from the bar I had invited to my home) pointed at me and said, "yes, that is him! He is the guilty one."

Cindy—my bride, confidant and best friend—heard every word.

I began to doubt myself again. *Did I black out and do this?*

I walked out of the courtroom into the blaze of popping camera flashes. The next day, my face was spread over every newspaper in Hong Kong. Here I was in all my glory. Now, all my team in Hong Kong would know about me including the church members at the local branch I have been attending every week. (The calls and emails I received from my company's international executives humbled and strengthened me as well.)

Thursday and Friday, Samuel went to work. He was relentless. At the end of the day Friday, he told me I would not be testifying. I deferred to his judgment. He rested his case and the wait began.

There were issues with the prosecution's case. The lab results did not reveal any misconduct. The women had not gone to the police until three or four hours after the alleged assault—she'd gone for noodles with her friends first. They encouraged her to file the charges.

The jury came back in an hour.

The vote was 6 to 1.

Not guilty.

I have never told this story—I was ashamed. Now I realize I should take pride in my innocence and in my tenacity. But, more important, I know I changed, and I know my transformation was due, in large measure, to Cindy's extraordinary courage and to the unlimited grace with which she showered me.

The next day, Cindy and I were on a plane headed for home.

CHAPTER 16
THE MERGER

When the calendars were approaching "2000," emotions ran the gamut from bemusement about the possibility of computer malfunctions to outright panic about the electronic breakdown of modern society. Y-2K panic was everywhere.

When the big ball fell on Park Avenue, nothing crashed, there was no Old Testament destruction and life went on pretty much the way it had been on December 31, 1999.

But, my Y-2K moment…my Armageddon…arrived as I sat at the breakfast table the morning of May 1, 2000. I was answering a routine voicemail when I heard a broadcast from Damon DeSantis, CEO of Rexall Sundown, our parent company, His announcement hit me like a sack of wet flour.

Rexall Sundown had been bought by a conglomerate from the Netherlands—Royal Numico. As RM had already bought GNC in March, the most recent acquisition made Royal Numico the largest manufacturer and distributor of nutritional products in the world.

I could not believe what I was hearing. Now, Enrich International and Rexall Showcase were owned by the same company. My thoughts started to race. *What's going to happen? How can you successfully manage two different companies, with two different compensation plans, two different cultures, two different management teams, and two different offices in each of the countries where they operate?*

The answer was clear—they couldn't. There would have to be a merger. "Why would a public company, whose sole focus is bottom line profits, operate two different offices, maintain two General Managers, utilize two different distribution facilities and so on in each country of operation?

Of course, the phone lines were burning up. The higher ups called everyone with the "everything will be fine" line—but you can't sell to a seller. I knew a smoke screen when I saw one. I'd been involved in mergers in the home building industry and nothing ever worked the way everyone thought it would. Only one culture would survive this. Productive activity came to a screeching halt and everyone wondered about the future—about their futures.

In retrospect, I don't think anyone had the vaguest clue. We, the MLM divisions of both parent companies, were an insignificant part of a bigger picture. The bottom line is that Numico had no North American business. It purchased GNC for the retail network and then purchased Rexall Sundown for manufacturing and manufacturing contracts with Wal-Mart, K-Mart and others. Again, the MLM businesses were an insignificant issue to Numico. They both just came along with the deal. None of us from the MLM divisions wanted to believe that but I feel this is the truth.

I'll be as objective as possible. Enrich International was fairly strong in Malaysia and especially strong in Japan due to the NFR program the company supported. The Japan business for Enrich was a major cash cow. Rexall Showcase had strength in the US, Hong Kong, Taiwan and relatively moderate success in Japan. All totaled the Enrich Business, due in very large measure to the Japan sales, was a bit bigger than the RSI business. We were told that the CEO of this newly formed MLM division would be the CEO of Enrich, R. B. Well that did not set well with the RSI people. It felt as if we were being merged with Enrich and heaven forbid that. We had very strong personalities at RSI in the USA and the lines in the sand began to be drawn. Oh, what a battle this ended up being over a three-year period. In essence the battle ended up being the sales of Japan, which meant the kowtowing to the Japanese leaders because of the almighty dollar. Looking back one can clearly see that principles and values were overlooked because the sales seemed more important. It was a monumental mistake and did great violence to my organization, which accounted for more than 70% of the RSI sales in Japan.

At the time of the merger, RSI's Japan Division generated $5 million (US) per month. As I write this, I am aware of what has happened to my monthly sales in Japan—a nosedive from $2 million a month to $125,000. In the same time period, Enrich's sales we from $16 million to $5 million per month. As the old comic strip *Pogo* said: "I have met the enemy and he is us."

> In the first few months, the Rexall CEO, D.S., remained quiet, but not R. B.. The Enrich people knew everything— if we wanted to know something, we asked someone from Enrich. It became obvious that Enrich was steering the ship.

One by one, the RSI people on the corporate side drifted away—most with generous severance deals. D. S., RSI CEO, left as well—his stock options burning a hole in his pocket. We heard a lot of things, but above all, the message consistently reminded us that we were going to remain two distinct companies.

Two years later, it all changed—new company—new name: Unicity Network. The folks in Japan resisted; they did not want to be known as Unicity and they did not want to follow the compensation plan. And here, the company "screwed the pooch" and chased the dollar instead of setting the directive and announcing, "No, we are Unicity Network—everywhere."

Not what happened.

The Enrich distributors were fighting over the Rexall folks. "Bring your entire team to the Enrich side" or "Rexall is doomed, come on over," or "We are poised for great growth."

It was a horrible time. The Enrich Nippon folks were doing whatever they wanted. Sure, that division had strong sales numbers—a veritable cash cow, and no one wanted to foul that up. But, the selection of sales over values and principles will eventually bite you in the butt.

The RSI IBO force was typified by chaos and dissention. Every month, we lost sales—and we lost people. Cross sponsoring became a major issue; significant organizations showed up under the Enrich side that were largely facilitated by some company staff at the Tokyo office. Even when we uncovered these situations, corrective action came with the speed of a water buffalo stuck in the mud. I could not understand the nature of the dilemma. Even though the situation was crystal clear (at least to me), no one seemed to know what to do.

I was stunned by the unacceptable, duplicitous behavior. Confidence eroded almost overnight. (Policies and procedures are all that protects an IBO—without them, it's the wild west.)

I am not saying anything was done with malice. But, no one minded the store and eventually, the entire business collapsed.

After months of heated debate (and legal action), the entire line was moved back to my group. But, the damage had been done. The total sales line sunk from $500k to $175k a month and the downward spiral continues. There were missing sales numbers—some people did not get their commissions.

The disaster was orchestrated, or at least overseen, by staff. It's just a great example of what happens when you stop following your rulebook.

In addition to all the vicissitudes of any merger, we had the bright idea of changing the compensation plan. Not satisfied, we changed it several times to the flavor of the month. When you alter the manner by which you pay people (the measuring stick they use), everyone has to re-learn "how to make money." After three years and dozens of training trips since the first change, some people still cannot figure it out. Some people think their checks are down because the plan stinks.

Truth is, sales were down—by more than half. If we wanted to get back to where we were, we had to rebuild the business. I thought I understood the plan very well. Our team followed a scheme designed to maximize everyone's income. I was confident the next year would prove our method correct.

Time would tell.

Two years into the merger, things settled a bit. I heard less and less about "Enrich and Rexall." We were becoming Unicity and we were all getting along like decent stepchildren can do. Bonds and friendships were beginning to develop, and both sides were seeing the value that the other brought to the table. We were getting back to business.

December 2002—another bombshell. Royal Numico announced its intent to divest of Rexall Sundown and Unicity Network. For many, it was the last straw. They started looking for somewhere else to work.

The next day, R. B. was in New York looking for a new buyer. They wanted a group of venture capitalists willing to buy the company at a huge discount, turn things around and take it public.

That's not what the IBO's wanted. We wanted an owner or ownership group because it was clear to us that publicly listed companies and MLM do not play well together. Someone needed to purchase the company lock, stock and barrel. Speculation danced all over the place in December and January.

"These things take time."

"No one spend millions at the drop of a hat."

"They have to look at the records and understand the financials—have some patience."

We hear rumors and then rumors about rumors. Truth was—no one knew anything.

Finally, February brought the news that Activated Holdings had entered into an agreement with Numico to purchase Unicity. Roger and Victor Barnett were the principals. Victor was from old English money, had begun with Revlon and later bought Burberry, turning it into the amazing company that is it today. He is a Branding Expert; his family is worth billions. His thirty-nine-year-old son, Roger—handsome, well-educated, entrepreneurial with astounding drive—was amicable and humble. The IBO force could not believe how lucky we were to have this turn of events.

I had met with Roger a few times; he even arranged a special meeting in Japan with me, my group and the leaders. He became very involved with the company.

All this took place *before* the deal was consummated. I was a little bit intrigued why Numico would let someone work inside the company and have so much access to resources and operations when they had not closed the purchase. They only had entered into an agreement. Nonetheless, it was Unicity's decision.

Roger and Victor were running the show for more than 4 months. The deal was announced to close end of June. Cindy and I received a special "all expenses paid" invitation to join Roger and Victor at the swanky Ritz Carlton resort in Ft. Lauderdale. Top leaders from all over the country from both Enrich and Rexall were to meet and have a glorious three days at the resort to wine and dine with the Barnetts.

In the limo on the way to the resort, I got a call from S. H.

"You sitting down?" he asked.

"I'm in a limo—what's up? Everything okay with your family?"

"Yes, but it's pretty serious."

"Spill it."

As S.H. talked, I could hear the pulse in my ears growing stronger—this was unbelievable.

"I just got off the phone with our friend T.S." he said. "The Barnetts are not buying. P. B. and A. W. closed on it this morning at 2 AM." "Is this verifiable?" I was fighting for calm.

"Call me when you get to the resort—I'll find out."

When Cindy and I got to the resort, we noticed two or three top leaders huddled in a corner with anxiety written all over their faces.

"I wonder if they already know," I thought.

We hurried to the room. Stewart answered on the first ring.

"It's true, Glade," he said. 'P.B. & A.W. now own Unicity."

I hung up and walked to the table by the window. There was an enormous welcome basket of fruits, crackers, cookies, mustards, cheeses along with other goodies and products. In an envelope hand-addressed to me was a personal note from Roger Barnett welcoming us to the event. The theme for the three days was "It's a new day."

No kidding.

Here's what I know:

- End of February 2003, Numico entered into an agreement with Activated Holdings (The Barnett Family) for the purchase of Unicity Network.

- The Barnetts took an active part in Unicity—sort of like letting potential buyers move into your house and redecorate before you close the deal.

- The closing date was scheduled for the end of June. No extension was ever signed. We were at the "It's a New Day" event in Florida in mid-July.

- P.B. had resigned as Chief Legal Officer of the company in May of 2003.

- July 1, 2003 The Numico CEO contacted P.B. to investigate possible interest in buying the company. P. B. (by reports) was working in his garden and stunned to receive the call.

- Approximately two weeks later, **P. B. & A.W.**, having demonstrated the ability to meet the same requirements as the Barnetts, consummate the deal and purchase Activated Holdings.

Here's what I *suspect*:

- Activated made a deal, then kept asking Numico for more and more of *this*—or a change in *that*.

- Numico took all it could and grew weary of the delaying tactics.

- Numico decides "the juice aint worth the squeeze" and calls P.B.

- The rest is history.

The next three days presented an interesting case study in human behavior. I saw every human emotion from anger…to hostility…to euphoria. The majority of those in attendance felt "duped." We were all in Florida to meet the new owners, but when the time came, a different owner popped out of the cake.

P. B. & A. W. met with most of the attendees in private, small group meetings where they tried to explain, face-to-face, exactly what happened. The new owners face extreme scrutiny by many of the IBO's. After all, we had been sold the Barnett/multi-million family story for several months. We'd lapped up how they'd turned Burberry into a multi-billion-dollar operation and what they were going to do with Unicity. I still believe the Barnett family really wanted Unicity—I think they were willing to go through with the deal. I suspect they blew a chance to own a great company with a rich heritage and strong, resilient and talented IBO's coupled with great products. An amalgamation of products and experienced IBO's of this nature is difficult to assemble.

Nonetheless, by the end of the time in Florida, P.B. & A. W. satisfied most everyone. The consensus was, "They are telling the truth."

This was not some underhanded deal. They were not looking to buy the company, then sell it for a quick million after a few weeks. No, they sincerely wanted to own it. This was their chance and I liked the fact they were willing to go "all in"—to put their homes, pensions, futures and trust funds at risk.

I know I make better decisions when I have something on the line. CEO's of public companies have very little skin in the game. They are watching the company on behalf of the shareholders. While they may draw huge salaries, they have very little personal exposure.

In my opinion, the reason MLM businesses do not work well as public companies is because the CEO has firm footing. The ice may be slippery, but it is thick.

It had been a bumpy and bizarre ride. Some people ended up with hurt feelings. Others remained suspicious. But, I really liked that P.B. & A. W. were willing to sink or swim with Unicity.

Even though they eventually…sank.

CHAPTER 17
CRUISIN' ALONG

The top rung in my business was "Royal Diamond' status. I wanted it more than a shortstop wants to spit. Halfway was never a goal—I shot for the top.

Three years after my wake-up call in Hong Kong, with my personal ship righted and my course clear, I had Royal Diamond in my sights.

I met Alan Ho when he was twenty-six. As soon as he signed on, the activity level escalated. He was destined for Royal Diamond status. He *went after it.* I quit counting the number of times he called at 5:00 AM (Hong Kong time)—he had not even gone to bed. He was the first Royal Diamond in the greater China region and I was proud of him.

Alan had two beautiful people in his downline who were knocking down records as fast as they could set them—Tiger and Michelle. Alan's English was good—Tiger and Michelle's, not so much. And my Mandarin is non-existent.

Despite the language barrier, Tiger and Michelle and I were totally in sync. We enjoyed a quiet, confident connection and held a strong mutual respect. I enjoyed working with them. They qualified for Royal Diamond one month after Alan achieved the mark.

No one had reached the Royal Diamond plateau in the previous two years. The Unicity world was expanding—all the IBO's were excited and enjoying success in China.

Alan, Tiger and Michelle had come on board when most of the other associates were wringing their hands and wondering if Paulo and Aaron were going to make a go of things. Instead of worrying, the "Three Amigos" hit the ground running. Their example inspired me.

I made it, too. I reached the pinnacle of Unicity's compensation plan. With the accolade, I received a bonus check for $100,000.

Tiger, Michelle and Alan showed me how to succeed. When everyone else is running around in panic and fear, if you put your head down and focus on business, you can do great things—even when other people are stumbling.

Zig Ziglar says, "If you help enough people get what they want then you will get what you want." Here's an example.

Tiger picked me up at the airport one day. He was with a few other folks. We walked outside and piled into an older truck. I sat in the back as we *whizzed* down the highway at 40 MPH. We were swaying like one of those inflatable air dancers outside a tire store. Cars zoomed past.

Everyone—except me—was speaking Chinese. They were laughing—except the driver. He seemed "heavy." Despite not understanding the language, I can read people.

We arrived at the meeting and had a good day. I had not given another thought to the ride in the truck.

Six months later, at an event in Hong Kong, I recognized the guy who'd been driving. Through a translator, he told me, "I was very excited to pick you up. Tiger had spoken so highly of you. But, I was embarrassed by my truck. It was all I could afford. I have done well with the company—now I have a beautiful car. Next time you come to my city, I want to pick you up, so you can see it."

I gave him a hug. "Your vehicle does not matter," my friend," I said. "People matter." I wanted him to know one of my core beliefs: Companies do not make people—people make companies.

I was grateful he shared the story. Seeing people better themselves drives me. Whenever I feel down, I remember how great he looked when he told me about his new vehicle.

Frank Lin's Taiwan team pushed me over the top—they are a great collection of humble, hard-working folks.

On one occasion, we needed to travel to another city. I assumed we would fly—I could afford it. Instead, we rode a "sleeping bus" all night long. I decided to do what the locals were doing. Being in the trenches with your people is important.

Instead of seats, the bus was filled with beds—one bed, an aisle—two beds, an aisle—one more bed, one more aisle. Oh—and all the beds were "double decker."

I got a better night's sleep than I anticipated. We arrived at 6 AM, checked in, freshened up and went to our meeting. The trip was a blast!

It may sound weird, but I get a bigger kick out of other people's success than I do out of my own. I am very grateful for what I have been able to accomplish, but I find excitement in the journey—not in the destination. The journey is what keeps me up at night—and what gets me out of bed in the morning.

I've slept on trains, crowded into airplanes, and sat through more meetings than I care to remember. One truth remains constant: regardless of where we work, what we wear, how we communicate, or how much we may (or may not) accumulate, we are all strikingly similar. A recent research brief from Stanford University reveals that all human beings are 99.9% the same. We have hopes, carry fears, and chase our dreams.

We live in a marvelous time. Technology continues to shrink the world. If we choose, we can be better connected and more intimately acquainted. How fortunate we are to possess the power to travel and to develop loving, caring relationships all over the world.

The future is bright—especially when we decide to engage.

From Sugar Beets to Shanghai

CHAPTER 18
TUMBLING DOWN

S. H. 's voice was calm and confident. "Glade, effective today, I have bought the company. I am the CEO and majority stockholder."

S. H. was my mentor and sponsor—he'd been my confidant for many years.

"Why?" I asked. "You have a great life. You work out of your home. The only time you're not in jeans and a tee-shirt, you are in your pajamas. Have you lost your mind?"

S. H. chuckled at the other end. "Thanks for the vote of confidence!"

The company was in financial ruins. P. B. & A. W. had never run so much as a lemonade stand. They bought Unicity from Royal Numico in a classic case of "How hard could this be?" They had sold off the real estate holdings and burned through millions of dollars. They'd funded commissions by borrowing money—mostly from S. H.. In truth, S. H. assumed control mostly to protect his own money.

I have to be cautious here (there is a Non-disclosure Agreement in place). In short, for reasons disclosed only to those involved, one-by-one, the company and many of the top leaders were in litigation. What happened was perfectly legal. We'd all signed documents we never thought would come into play. One-by-one, commission checks were suspended. The burden of proof fell to the producer who had to prove that he or she was entitled to the compensation. In one case, the distributor spent $500,000 over eight years trying to fight the battle. Most of the folks at Unicity did not have that kind of money.

They'd made fantastic—borderline ridiculous—money, but you tend to spend to your limits. Very few people had enough cash in reserve to engage in a protracted legal dispute.

I testified—numerous times—as a favor to the company. The allegations against the distributors were true—I never lied. But, I never suspected that I would soon be on the other side of the courtroom trying to defend myself against the company.

When my day in court came, I was already into the attorneys for $25,000. On the way in to hear a summary judgment, I asked if there was a way to resolve the case amicably. I did not want the poison of contention running through my life.

My attorney wanted to fight; the CEO's attorney wanted to fight. I wanted to move on.

"I'm willing to walk away if we just drop everything," I said.

I agreed not to disparage the company if the other side would refrain from saying anything unkind about me.

Thirty minutes later, it was over.

The company retained my commission check and I had a new start.

I spent hundreds of thousands of hours and traveled millions of miles—for nothing.

It was all gone.

There's always next year.

CHAPTER 19
A DECADE LOST

We all would prefer easy lives.

But, where is the growth in that?

I was nearing my mid-50's. There had been incredible highs. I had been hoisted up on a platform in China in front of 5000 cheering, raucous onlookers. I'd enjoyed backstage "green room" experiences with CEO's, motivational speakers, top notch authors, writers and celebrities.

And, I'd walked "through the valley of the shadow"—wanting to swim toward the horizon until it and oblivion swallowed and submerged me. I'd made and lost millions—been a part of successful businesses and crushing failure. I'd participated in torpedoing a marriage but was fortunate enough to have found love and happiness again.

Bottom line—I was tired—tired of the chase—tired of hard work. Now, living in Idaho, I was in the middle of watching my fourteen-year business relationship with Unicity/Rexall dissolve like an Alka-Seltzer tablet in water. The destructive gears of the Great Recession were beginning to mesh—economic disaster loomed. I'd already seen this cycle three times—build equity—watch it go *pssfft!*

It was a great time to begin a decade-long pity party—a ten-year funk where confidence evaporated and *stinkin' thinkin'* flourished.

Was I supposed to learn something? Again? How was I in this situation one more time? What was I missing?

In my heart, I felt I was holding true to faith; I was serving where and how I could. I worked to be a good neighbor and to live the golden rule. How could God keep doing this to me? I'd always believed that my trust, belief and fidelity would result in blessing. Isn't that the promise? We'd busted it—we'd been kind—we'd lived good lives—we'd prospered and built the house of a lifetime. Now we were in a rental with a bank account full of squat and a future full of dust.

I joined another company in the MLM world and was surrounded by some very talented people, but I never was 100 % on fire because of my self-doubts. Questions pounded me—by the day…by the hour… by the minute. Things looked promising for a while. Then, my business partner was diagnosed with cancer. The business stalled while she fought bravely, then crumbled after she lost her battle.

My attempts at restarting the business were about as successful as resuscitating a dead gerbil. Another company acquired us for pennies on the dollar.

This was like a bad game of Whack-a-Mole. The very issues that wrecked my previous construction and MLM enterprises were popping up again. Self-doubt slowly tightened its icy grip on my throat. I wondered about the reality of success.

Was stability a theory—something we see in movies—or could I achieve it?

I returned to square one, acquiring an Idaho contractor's license and building houses again. The drive wasn't there—I didn't have any juice. I was not the Lone Ranger—better business minds than mine lost everything, but my struggle was *mine* and every setback—large or small—put another dent in what little belief I still had in myself. While I never approached the emotional depths of my experience at Hong Kong Bay, I was sinking fast.

My attitude went south. Customers can always be challenging, but I'd always been able to deal with their demands. After all, a home is a serious investment and people want the best—they expect and deserve bang for their buck. Any man-made project will have flaws, and I always did everything *humanly possible* to fix any defect in workmanship or quality.

With a million moving parts, nothing about a construction project goes exactly according to plan. I began to see customers as "them"—the enemy. Didn't "they" know how hard I worked? I spent money on a better footing, so your house would not sink due to a high-water table. I shaved my profit margin by constructing a better foundation. Heck, I put heaters (covered with blankets) on your new driveway to keep it from freezing and cracking.

And all they did was bitch and moan. One little scratch…one little nail pop…one little *anything*…it was always the "worst job they'd ever seen."

In reality, my customers were great—my nerves were raw, and I was close to throwing in the towel. After building over thirty homes, I was miserable.

But, hope rose on the horizon of my despair in the form of my darling wife. With only one child left at home (a high school senior), Cindy launched a real estate career. She sought out the best training in the country and went to a seminar in Dallas to learn from a group of the best team-building agents in the business. Their system generated significant, positive results.

While I plowed deeper into despair and self-pity, Cindy busted it, adapted the principles she'd learned and chased her own dream. Her business started to thrive.

I'm embarrassed to admit it, but as great as it was to watch her soar, at the same time, her achievement hacked away at the roots of what little self-esteem I had left. Earlier, Cindy had *poo-pooed* Zig Ziglar, Jim Rohn, and other personal growth and development gurus I admired.

Now, she was listening to them, implementing their philosophies and practices, and kicking my self-absorbed behind. What the $&*#?

Now, she was the big shot—the success. While Mr. Mom stayed at home with the teenager and the dog, Cindy rode out of the castle in search of dragons to slay. While I was whining, she was winning!

Cindy rose to the top three percent in her industry. She obtained her broker's license. She was earning thirteen times the national average for her profession. I didn't mind the cooking and the cleaning but asking for an allowance shriveled my ego.

One of her coaches was Brian Buffini, the number one business mentor in North America. Cindy knew I was despondent, and she wanted to help. But, she was cagey enough to understand that I had to decide to change. Pity and poking were not going to solve anything.

On a Saturday morning while Cindy was out of town, I listened to one of Brian's podcasts. I only listened because she asked. The August 14, 2018 podcast was entitled "How to Be Resilient." Brian was talking directly to me. I listened to the same podcast five times before Cindy returned.

He'd "read my mail." He described my condition, my ten-year funk, my disappointment, my discouragement, my depression…exactly. He told stories about Thomas Edison, Vincent Van Gogh, J.C.Penney and Henry Ford. He related J.K. Rowling's struggles—living on the streets and writing—turned down by eleven publishers before unleashing the worldwide sensation of Harry Potter. Jim Carey, Steven Spielberg, Colonel Sanders…example after example about how bankruptcy, divorce, and repeated mistakes lost their power in the face of resilience.

What had they done differently? They'd kept going. They'd been hit in the face with disappointment, discouragement and depression, and they'd gone forward. No one mentioned their failures now because they'd overwhelmed everything with their achievements.

The message was familiar—I'd heard it for decades. But, this time, it resonated—and I was fired up!

I immersed myself in Brian Buffini's podcasts. I started reading good books again. I realized my passion was for helping others. Slowly, I started to change my inner focus to an outer drive, using the enduring principles I'd learned throughout life to help other people.

Newton's Laws of Physics are immutable. So are basic principles. Decency is like gravity—it does not change, and it has irresistible power.

Once again, Cindy had reached into the swamp of my personal despair, grabbed me by the collar and said, "Oh no you don't, Mister."

In *The Greatest Salesman in the World*, Og Mandino says: "I will persist until I succeed." That became my new mantra. I repeated it at least twenty times a day. And I repeat it still.

I *will* persist until I succeed.

CHAPTER 20
HALF-FULL OR HALF-EMPTY?

In *The Next Millionaires*, Paul Zane Pilzer defines the law of scarcity as, "Believing that there is only a limited amount of money, air, fuel, and other vital resources in the world."

When we believe in the limits, our natural reaction is to fight—to get what we want and need (including money) and to keep it for ourselves. If things are limited, not everyone can have enough—and *we must have enough.*

Pilzer continues, "When you begin with this assumption of scarcity, it's not hard to see where this thinking soon leads. If there is a limited supply, what do you do when you are running out? You go next door, kill the people in the next village, and take theirs. That is the history of war. It is dressed up with all sorts of rhetoric, justification and complexity, but it really boils down to that."

As history demonstrates, the great economic powers of the Western World have derived their wealth and economic might from the practice of relatively unfettered free trade—something Pilzer would see and the antidote to armed conflict.

In the years following World War II, both Germany and Japan quickly became vigorous trading partners with the United States; soon they were major economic powers themselves. Now, it seems highly unlikely that the U.S. would go to war with Germany or Japan or vice versa.

I have been working in and around Asia for the past three decades. China stands as a shining example of Pilzer's theory. Thirty years ago, just about the only vehicles on the streets were taxis. The other night in

Shenzhen, it took me two hours to travel what would have taken thirty minutes twenty years ago. The sheer number of vehicles is astounding.

Mission Hills in Shenzhen boasts the Guinness World Record for the largest golf complex on the planet—ten, 18-hole courses laid out by the world's best designers. Huge homes dot the landscape around the tracks—the landscaping is stunning. Each home costs about seven million dollars (US)—and they were completely sold out before the first dwelling was completed.

What astounding wealth!

China is a massive trading partner with the world. In a very controlled and deliberate fashion, she has opened her borders to global companies like Unicity. Chairman Mao must be spinning in his grave—a Communist country with burgeoning, non-Chinese-controlled business enterprises.

Moreover, even American farm boys like me can share in the bounty China generates. What Mr. Pilzer states is true. If we create great trading relationships with others, there is no scarcity. There is only abundance.

Abundance means enough for everyone—no finite amount of wealth and opportunity. When we trade with other people, we create indestructible bonds.

Governments wage wars.

People build peace.

Free trade is the engine that fuels the growth of wealth. It reduces the selfish, human impulses that lead to savage hostility.

Coupled with free trade, individual ownership creates a transformative force that works to everyone's benefit. When you own your own business, everything affects you—peace and tranquility benefits what you do—strife and pain reduces your chances of success.

The only limits to the human mind are self-imposed. What we conceive …we believe…then, we achieve.

CHAPTER 21
NO SUCH WORD

These stories are all real. Sharing them with you is not the easiest thing I have ever done. But, I want my honesty and openness to help you to understand yourself, your strengths, your weaknesses—and to be courageous.

When I was young and working on the farm, I always tried to get out of doing something I either did not want to do or was afraid to try. "Dad, I can't," was my go-to phrase.

The reply never varied. "No such word as 'can't', son."

I hated when he said that. Now, sixty-plus years later, I smile when I think about it, because I know he was right.

The only limitations we have are self-imposed.

As I stated in the forward of this book, my intent is to inspire you to live your life to the fullest. Dream big and have the tenacity to endure the challenges that *will come*. Fail forward to the realization of your goals and dreams. Beware of the dream-stealers and naysayers. We all are endowed with the seeds of greatness. As the saying goes, "God don't make junk," and we were not sent here to live in complacency and mediocrity. I really believe that.

> *"Whatever you do, or dream you can, begin it. Boldness has genius and power and magic in it."*
> *– Johan Wolfgang Goethe*

However, nothing ever seems to go as easily or perfectly as we imagine, but *what* we do and *how* we face challenges and difficulties in the midst of those challenges defines who we are and define our character.

Jim Rohn says it this way: "In the process of living, the winds of circumstances blow on us all in an unending flow that touches each of our lives." What guides us to different destinations in life is determined by the course we choose when we set our sail. The way you think makes the major difference in where you will arrive. (Mindset)

We all have difficulties, disappointments and challenges. Fortunes rise and fall in an instant. Sometimes, despite meticulous planning and monumental effort, things just seem to fall apart. In the final analysis, it is not what happens that determines the quality of our lives; it is what we do when we have set our course and the wind changes directions. (Habits)

As you know by now, I have been disappointed, discouraged and, yes, even depressed at times. In Hong Kong I wanted to jump into the ocean, but my good wife talked me through "the dark night of the soul" until a new day dawned. I had a decade of discouragement where I lost confidence in myself and experienced mediocre business results, at best. But thanks to the words of encouragement of a podcast and Cindy's trust and confidence in me, I found my way to new hope and pointed the vessel of my life in a new direction. (Routines)

Three key patterns can change your direction:

- Mindset
- Habits
- Routines

There are a plethora of self-help and development books out there with each of these.

- **Mindset:** When I became a voracious student of success, personal growth and development in my early twenties, there were not a lot of available resources. Now, you can find almost limitless books, podcasts, seminars, webinars and events. Information comes at us like water from a firehose, but we are thirsting for wisdom. Today, anyone can author a book (even me), start a blog or post something inspirational and become a self-proclaimed expert. But not everyone asks the tough questions:

- Where have you been?
- What have you built?
- What have you really done?

These questions will reveal the real story. Warren Buffet said it this way, "Only when the tide goes out do you discover who's been swimming naked!" Be careful who you listen to, what you read and what you watch.

There are three ways to influence your mind:

- **Read:** Mark Twain once commented, "The man who does not read good books has no advantage over the man who cannot read them."

  Reading is the highest form of retention. There is a neurological connection between reading and our brains. Psychologists have found that "Reading has the power to reshape your brain and improve theory of mind" and yet forty-two percent of graduates never read a book after graduating from college. We look at our smart phones, on average, over forty-six times a day. Millennials take a glance seventy-six times a day. We *touch* our phones on average 2,617 times a day and yet we *read* very little. Fewer than five percent of Americans read on a regular basis and yet reading represents the skill (or mindset) most likely to spark the impetus for change. You want to change your life? *Read* the right stuff, *listen* to the right stuff and *watch* the right stuff.

- **Listen:** Listening is the second most impactful thing you can do to change your life. What you listen to matters. Turn your commute to work, your runs, your walks, your TV time into "audioversity" and it will change your life. Listen to some head banging music and see where that gets you! Then, try a symphony by Beethoven. Mix it up. There is so much good stuff out there. I started off listening to audio cassette tapes, then CDs, and now podcasts while driving around. Our Danish exchange student from thirty-five years ago still laughs about our doing 100 MPH on the back roads of Wyoming while listening to motivational cassette tapes. He immigrated to the US and owns a chain of movie and camera accessories stores. He attributes a lot of his success to the inspiration he gleaned from the tapes. They helped him set his sail on living a dream of immigrating to (and living in) the US where he could escape Scandinavia's small economic market.

- **Watch:** I don't watch the news. CNN has a different acronym to me than Cable News Network. I call it "Crisis News Network." If you listen to the news, you would think the sky is falling. According to newscasters, all the people in the world are sketchy criminals. "Negativity sells" and the media has to raise advertising revenue, so they focus on the negative. Don't waste your time. Recently I was in Japan and we were in the heart of Tokyo. There was a lot of congestion; the trains were not running on time. My colleague said, "Oh, it is because President Trump is in Tokyo." "He is?" I said, "He didn't tell me he was coming here!" My friend laughed. I had no idea he would be so intrigued that I did not know. After I told him I did not watch the news, I launched into my lesson on what to read, what to listen to and what to watch. Don't get me wrong. I love watching movies. *Rudy* is probably my all-time favorite movie. Why? Because, I'm Rudy—and you can be as well. Og Mandino said it this way: "I will persist until I succeed." That has been my mantra since my early twenties. There is no such word as "can't." Now, have I always lived it? Did I practice what I preach? Not always, but I have tried to most of the time. Anyone who knows me will say I am an optimist. Do I have bad days? Absolutely—as I have shared. I had a horrible decade. but I will persist until I succeed.

Let's talk about habits.

Formulating a dream, setting goals, and writing down your vision are some of the best habits you can develop if you are chasing success. In *7 Habits of Highly Successful People*, Steven R. Covey calls it "Beginning with the end in mind." Where do you want to go? What do you want to achieve? What does your character look like, feel like and what will you become? Without a Vision and a Plan, you may tread a lot of water, but you won't make any forward progress. Goals and dreams make things happen. They give you a target—they raise anticipation and excitement. When you get discouraged or hear a disparaging remark, when the dream-stealers are screaming in your mind, and/or you are dog dead tired and you want to stop, your dreams…your goals…your vision motivate you to "get up and win that race." One of my favorite poems, and I have it walled in front of me in my office, is entitled "Invictus."

Out of the night that covers me,
Black as the pit from pole to pole,
I thank whatever gods may be
For my unconquerable soul.

In the fell clutch of circumstance
I have not winced nor cried aloud.
Under the bludgeonings of chance
My head is bloody, but unbowed.

Beyond this place of wrath and tears
Looms but the Horror of the shade,
And yet the menace of the years
Finds and shall find me unafraid.

It matters not how strait the gate,
How charged with punishments the scroll,
I am the master of my fate,
I am the captain of my soul.

~ William Ernest Henley

Without goals, without vision, without purpose, we become complacent. We take no risks; we manage the status quo. Bottom line—you are either moving forward and up—or backward and down. Jim Collins, in *Good to Great* says, "Good is the enemy of great." All successful people wage a daily war against complacency. Their DNA contains the habits of goal setting and aspiring to be more, to serve more and to help others accomplish more. It is the essence of servant leadership.

No one can lead from a position of weakness. Leadership is chosen by the people; real servant leadership is about building yourself first and then showing others how you did it. Real leaders build other leaders.

How do you eat an elephant? One bite at a time. That's not sexy, but it is true. And it holds true for dreams, visions, and goals. Believe in yourself and focus on the three things I learned from famed coach Lou Holtz:

- Do the right thing and avoid the wrong thing. (Mindset)
- Commit to an attitude of excellence—do the best you can and don't settle for anything less than excellence. (Habits)
- Show people you care about them. (Routines)

We all find ourselves motivated by an event, a great book, a good movie or powerful podcast, but after a few days, the "want to" goes *pssssfft*—like air out of a leaky tire. Why? Because *inspiration* (while powerful and necessary) never takes the place of *planning*.

Think about Zig Ziglar's comment:

> *Of course, motivation is not permanent, but then, neither is bathing; but it is something we should do on a regular basis.*

The planning you put on your vision board, your dream board, will continually feed your motivation. Keep it in front of you all the time.

Post visual, written affirmations.

I like to use the acronym W-I-N.

It stands for *What's Important Now.*

Ask yourself the question at least twenty-five times a day—every single day.

Your focus will take on a razor's edge and you will be astounded at what you *will* accomplish.

And remember, whether you think you can, or you can't—you're right.

EPILOGUE

Thank you for reading (or listening to) *From Sugar Beets to Shanghai*. My dearest wish is that it will give you hope and the courage to face your personal battles.

Giving up is easy. Persistence is hard.

But, staying with it pays off. Your determination to "make it" will see you through whatever tough times you encounter.

I hope our paths cross some day and, until that happens, may God be with you. Don't ever give up.

There is no such word as "can't."

Go Forward with Faith

Anyone who believes that life is a bed of roses or sitting on the island with umbrella drinks will spend a lot of time running around thinking they have been robbed.

Not all your putts don't fall.

Our teams don't win every championship.

Rags to riches stories belong to Hollywood.

Our children are most likely not going to set records in any professional sports arena.

Marriage requires work, sacrifice and tolerance.

Still, we have a say—a big one. We can create our future…good or bad. We have a choice.

I *chose* to wander in a funk for ten years. I *chose* to feel sorry for the bad breaks, the stupid decisions, economic downturns, and personal *Hindenburg* disasters. I *chose* to feel that my past accomplishments entitled me to bliss.

I also *chose* to waste one of life's most fleeting commodities—time.

And, I have *chosen* to change. I cannot rewrite the past and I cannot alter the future, but I can surely help shape my present. I live in the now…I make good choices (in consultation with wise advisors and those I love, respect and who are impacted by what I do)…I spend my time wisely…I employ healthy habits designed to create positive results.

I *choose* to replace pessimism with an upward look…to move destructive behavior out and to invite productive routines in. I live by the law of the harvest—I put out quality…and I reap it back a thousand-fold.

Holding onto low self-esteem means you will go through life while you are pulling on the handbrake. You burn a lot of rubber…you don't make a lot of progress. The greatest entrepreneurial investment you can make…is in yourself.

I *choose* to live as a person of faith. What I believe directs how I live and while it cannot possibly guard me from all disappointment, my faith shields me against depression, discouragement, and crippling self-deprecation.

How does the old saying go? "God don't make no junk."

The mistakes come, not from the Designer but from the "designed." Operator error will always be the leading cause of human suffering, tragedy, and loss.

I *choose* to believe that I was not put here to fail.

Life will not be easy.

But, still, I *choose!*

ACKNOWLEDGEMENTS

No one get through life (successfully) in a vacuum. I need to thank a few people.

My heartfelt appreciation to…

Bob Saxton, my first boss, someone who believed in me from the beginning and continues to be a mentor and friend.

Dell Loy Hansen, you gave me my first chance out of college. You are a big thinker and my closest rags-to-riches colleague.

Ross Layton—the ultimate example of someone who remains true to his faith and his happiness while serving others even amidst personal challenges. Ross, you have helped and mentored me with grace and class.

Nathan Ricks—your coaching in the MLM world continues to inspire me. You are a giant of a man whose principles, patterns and processes for success I will always embrace.

John and Delores Dickson—these true servant leaders were pillars of strength to Cindy and me during my Hong Kong stay. They met with us and gave us hope, faith and an abiding understanding of Christian values, principles, comfort and faith.

Arthur Fogartie—my editor. Arthur, you have been a godsend. Your ability to rummage through piles of information, notes, stories, and my verbosity and to craft a coherent message is truly a remarkable skill. I could not have done this without you.

And to everyone else along this continuing journey—blessings and peace.

The Og Mandino Leadership Institute and Dave Blanchard, CEO of the foundation, have been instrumental to my personal growth and development in the past year! When I was in a funk, my thoughts were in a consistent ebb and flow of catastrophe! Always having systemic thoughts about everything that could go wrong any why they could or would create a personal disaster.

I hired Dave as a personal coach but he first had me take an assessment, unlike anything I had ever taken before, then he shared with me how my habits of thinking were being destructive and self defeating and that if I wanted to change my life then I must first change my thoughts! After understanding where my blind spots were, and we all have them, then I could take on my life and intentionally create a brighter future.

I offer you that same opportunity for free. Please visit this website and take the assessment. It measures your own habits of thinking. It takes about 20 minutes and you will be astounded at the accuracy! www.habitfindercoach.com/gladepoulsen is where you will find the assessment. Then, if you choose, I am happy to spend 1/2 hour explaining the measurements for a little deeper understanding.

Made in United States
Troutdale, OR
03/15/2025